3rd Workshop on The People's Web Meets NLP: Collaboratively Constructed Semantic Resources and Their Applications to NLP

Held at the 50th Annual Meeting of the Association for Computational Linguistics (ACL 2012)

Jeju, Republic of Korea
13 July 2012

ISBN: 978-1-62748-343-8

Printed from e-media with permission by:

Curran Associates, Inc.
57 Morehouse Lane
Red Hook, NY 12571

Some format issues inherent in the e-media version may also appear in this print version.

Printed by Curran Associates, Inc. (2013)

For permission requests, please contact the Association for Computational Linguistics at the address below.

Association for Computational Linguistics
209 N. Eighth Street
Stroudsburg, Pennsylvania 18360

Phone: 1-570-476-8006
Fax: 1-570-476-0860

acl@aclweb.org

Additional copies of this publication are available from:

Curran Associates, Inc.
57 Morehouse Lane
Red Hook, NY 12571 USA
Phone: 845-758-0400
Fax: 845-758-2634
Email: curran@proceedings.com
Web: www.proceedings.com

Introduction

Recent emergence of Collaboratively Constructed Semantic Resources has led to a set of new research topics that became visible at major computational linguistics conferences. Researchers have studied methods to utilize collaboratively constructed resources to substitute or supplement conventional lexical semantic and linguistically annotated resources. At the same time, Natural Language Processing techniques have been applied to enhance the collaboration process and the overall quality of the collaboratively constructed resources.

This volume contains papers accepted for presentation at the 3rd Workshop on Collaboratively Constructed Semantic Resources and their Applications to NLP, which took place on July 13, 2012, as part of the ACL 2012 conference in Jeju, Republic of Korea. We received submissions from a broad spectrum of research topics, going beyond the coverage of the previous workshops. After careful review by our program committee, three long papers and three short papers were finally accepted for presentation.

The preceding "People's Web meets NLP" workshops at ACL-IJCNLP 2009 and COLING 2010 have successfully gathered researchers from different areas and allowed an interdisciplinary exchange of research outcomes and ideas. The workshop has contributed to the creation of valuable semantic resources and tools based on Collaboratively Constructed Semantic Resources and the consolidation of this young research field.

As the third one in the series, this workshop aims to intensify research that demonstrates the effectiveness of the resources mined from Collaboratively Constructed Semantic Resources in diverse Natural Language Processing tasks. We issued a call for both long and short papers. We especially encouraged submissions that show the benefit of Collaboratively Constructed Semantic Resources in diverse Natural Language Processing tasks.

The aim of the People's Web Meets NLP workshop series is to bring together researchers with different backgrounds: from computational linguistics to various Natural Language Processing areas that benefit from collaboratively constructed semantic resources. We hope this is well reflected in the proceedings.

Jeju, July 2012

Iryna Gurevych, Nicoletta Calzolari Zamorani, and Jungi Kim

Organizers:

Iryna Gurevych, Ubiquitous Knowledge Processing Lab, Technische Universität Darmstadt
Nicoletta Calzolari Zamorani, Istituto di Linguistica Computazionale, CNR
Jungi Kim, Ubiquitous Knowledge Processing Lab, Technische Universität Darmstadt

Program Committee:

Andras Csomai, Google Inc.
Andreas Hotho, Julius-Maximilians-Universität Würzburg
Anette Frank, Heidelberg University
Benno Stein, Bauhaus University Weimar
Christian M. Meyer, Technische Universität Darmstadt
David Milne, University of Waikato
Delphine Bernhard, University of Strasbourg
Diana McCarthy, Lexical Computing Ltd, UK
Donald Metzler, Information Sciences Institute, University of Southern California
Emily Pitler, University of Pennsylvania
Ernesto William De Luca, Technische Universität Berlin
Florian Laws, University of Stuttgart
Gerard de Melo, UC Berkeley
German Rigau, University of the Basque Country
Graeme Hirst, University of Toronto
Günter Neumann, DFKI Saarbrücken
Ido Dagan, Bar Ilan University
John McCrae, University of Bielefeld
Jong-Hyeok Lee, Pohang University of Science and Technology
Judith Eckle-Kohler, Technische Universität Darmstadt
Magnus Sahlgren, Swedish Institute of Computer Science
Manfred Stede, Universität Potsdam
Massimo Poesio, University of Essex
Omar Alonso, Microsoft Bing
Paul Buitelaar, DERI, National University of Ireland, Galway
Rene Witte, Concordia University Montréal
Roxana Girju, University of Illinois at Urbana-Champaign
Saif Mohammad, National Research Council Canada
Shuming Shi, Microsoft Research
Sören Auer, Leipzig University
Tat-Seng Chua, National University of Singapore
Tonio Wandmacher, SYSTRAN, Paris, France
Zornitsa Kozareva, Information Sciences Institute, University of Southern California

Invited Speaker:

Massimo Poesio, University of Essex

Title: Phrase Detectives: the First Three Years

Abstract: Phrase Detectives, one of the first games-with-a-purpose for corpus annotation (`www.phrasedetectives.org`) went officially online on December 1st 2008, and one of its very first presentations in front of an NLP audience took place at the first edition of the "People's Web Meets NLP" workshop in Singapore in 2009. The option of annotating Italian documents was added in 2010, and a Facebook version went live in January 2012. Although the project that funded its creation ended in September 2009, the game has stayed very much alive, in fact it is getting more active all the time - we recently passed the 11,000 players mark and are about to reach 200,000 words of fully annotated documents, with a goal of annotating at least 1 million. In the talk I will discuss recent developments and analyze the results so far in terms of quality and quantity of annotated data and annotation costs.

References: Massimo Poesio, Jon Chamberlain, Udo Kruschwitz, Livio Robaldo, and Luca Ducceschi, In Press - Phrase Detectives: Utilizing Collective Intelligence for Internet-Scale Language Resource Creation, ACM Transactions on Interactive Intelligent Systems.

Short bio: Massimo Poesio is a Professor of Computer Science at the University of Essex and the Director of the Language Interaction and Computation Lab at the Centre for Mind/Brain Sciences, University of Trento. He is best known for his work in anaphora resolution, corpus annotation, and the acquisition of common sense knowledge.

Table of Contents

Workshop Program

Friday July 13, 2012

09:15–09:30 Opening remarks

09:35–10:05 *Sentiment Analysis Using a Novel Human Computation Game*
Claudiu Cristian Musat, Alireza Ghasemi and Boi Faltings

10:10–10:30 *A Serious Game for Building a Portuguese Lexical-Semantic Network*
Mathieu Mangeot and Carlos Ramisch

10:30–11:00 Coffee break

11:00–11:20 *Collaboratively Building Language Resources while Localising the Web*
Asanka Wasala, Reinhard Schäler, Ruvan Weerasinghe and Chris Exton

11:25–12:30 Invited talk: Phrase Detectives: The First Three Years by Massimo Poesio

12:30–14:00 Lunch break

14:00–14:30 *Resolving Task Specification and Path Inconsistency in Taxonomy Construction*
Hui Yang

14:35–15:55 *EAGER: Extending Automatically Gazetteers for Entity Recognition*
Omer Farukhan Gunes, Tim Furche, Christian Schallhart, Jens Lehmann and Axel-Cyrille Ngonga Ngomo

15:00–15:30 *Extracting Context-Rich Entailment Rules from Wikipedia Revision History*
Elena Cabrio, Bernardo Magnini and Angelina Ivanova

15:30–16:00 Coffee break

16:00–17:00 Panel discussion: Collaboratively Looking Ahead: How to Make Sustainable Goods out of Collaboratively Constructed Semantic Resources?

Sentiment Analysis Using a Novel Human Computation Game

Claudiu-Cristian Musat **Alireza Ghasemi** **Boi Faltings**

Artificial Intelligence Laboratory (LIA)
Ecole Polytechnique Fédérale de Lausanne (EPFL)
IN-Ecublens, 1015 Lausanne, Switzerland
firstname.lastname@epfl.ch

Abstract

In this paper, we propose a novel human computation game for sentiment analysis. Our game aims at annotating sentiments of a collection of text documents and simultaneously constructing a highly discriminative lexicon of positive and negative phrases.

Human computation games have been widely used in recent years to acquire human knowledge and use it to solve problems which are infeasible to solve by machine intelligence. We package the problems of lexicon construction and sentiment detection as a single human computation game. We compare the results obtained by the game with that of other well-known sentiment detection approaches. Obtained results are promising and show improvements over traditional approaches.

1 Introduction

We propose a novel solution for the analysis of sentiment expressed in text media. Novel corpus based and lexicon based sentiment analysis methods are created each year. The continual emergence of conceptually similar methods for this known problem shows that a satisfactory solution has still not been found. We believe that the lack of suitable labelled data that could be used in machine learning techniques to train sentiment classifiers is one of the major reasons the field of sentiment analysis is not advancing more rapidly.

Recognizing that knowledge for understanding sentiment is common sense and does not require experts, we plan to take a new approach where labelled data is obtained from people using human computation platforms and games. We also prove that the method can provide not only labelled texts, but people also help by selecting sentiment-expressing features that can generalize well.

Human computation is a newly emerging paradigm. It tries to solve large-scale problems by utilizing human knowledge and has proven useful in solving various problems (Von Ahn and Dabbish, 2004; Von Ahn, 2006; Von Ahn et al., 2006a).

To obtain high quality solution from human computation, people should be motivated to make their best effort. One way to incentivize people for submitting high-quality results is to package the problem at hand as a game and request people to play it. This process is called gamification. The game design should be such that the solution to the main problems can be formed by appropriately aggregating results of played games.

In this work, we propose a cooperative human computation game for sentiment analysis called Guesstiment. It aims at annotating sentiment of a collection of text documents, and simultaneously constructing a lexicon of highly polarized (positive and negative) words which can further be used for sentiment detection tasks. By playing a collaborative game, people rate hotel reviews as positive and negative and select words and phrases within the reviews that best express the chosen polarity.

We compare these annotations with those obtained during a former crowd-sourcing survey and prove that packaging the problem as a game can improve the quality of the responses. We also compare our approach with the state-of-the-art machine learning techniques and prove the superiority of human cognition for this task. In a third experiment we use the same annotations in a multi faceted opinion classification problem and find that results are superior to those obtained using known linguistic resources.

In (section 2) we review the literature related to our work. We then outline the game and its rules (section 3). We compare the Guesstiment results to the state-of-the-art machine learning, standard crowd-sourcing methods and sentiment dictionaries(section 4) and conclude the paper with ideas for future work (section 5).

2 Related Work

In this section we review the important literature related and similar to our work. Sine we propose a human computation approach for sentiment analysis, we start by reviewing the literature on human computation and the closely related field of crowd-sourcing. Then we move on by having a brief look on the human computation and knowledge acquisition games proposed so far by the researchers. Finally, we briefly review major sentiment analysis methods utilized by the researchers.

2.1 Human Computation and Crowd-Sourcing

The literature on human computation is highly overlapping with that of crowd-sourcing, as they are closely connected. The two terms are sometimes used interchangeably although they are slightly different. Crowd-sourcing in its broadest form, "is the act of taking a job traditionally performed by a designated agent (usually an employee) and outsourcing it to an undefined, generally large group of people in the form of an open call"(Quinn and Bederson, 2011; Howe, 2006). Since the first use of the word crowd-sourcing by J. Howe (Howe, 2006), there has been a lot of interest in this field due to the wide accessibility of anonymous crowd workers across the web.

The work described in (Rumshisky, 2011) uses crowd-sourcing to perform word sense disambiguation on a corpus. In (Vondrick et al., 2010), crowd-sourcing is used for video annotation. Moreover, (Christophe et al., 2010) has used crowd-sourcing for satellite image analysis.

(Settles, 2011a) is another approach which aims at combining active learning with crowd-sourcing for text classification. The principal contribution of their work is that as well as document annotation, they use human computation also to perform feature selection. (Law et al.,) is another recent work which proposes a game for acquisition of attribute-value pairs from images.

2.2 Human Computation Games

Luis Von Ahn, the pioneer of the field of human computation, designed a game to encourage players to semantically annotate a large corpus of images (Von Ahn and Dabbish, 2004). It was the first human computation game.

Following Von Ahn's work, more researchers were encouraged to package computational problems as joyful games and have a group of non-expert users play them (Von Ahn, 2006). Verbosity (Von Ahn et al., 2006a) was designed with the goal of gathering common sense knowledge about words. KissKissBan (Ho et al., 2009) was another game for image annotation.

Peekaboom(Von Ahn et al., 2006b) aimed at image segmentation and "Phrase Detectives" (Chamberlain et al., 2008) was used to help constructing an anamorphic corpus for NLP tasks. Another human computation game is described in (Riek et al., 2011) whose purpose is semantic annotation of video data.

2.3 Sentiment Analysis

The field of sentiment analysis and classification currently mostly deals with extracting sentiment from text data. Various methods (Turney, 2002; Esuli and Sebastiani, 2006; Taboada et al., 2011; Pang et al., 2002) have been proposed for effective and efficient sentiment extraction of large collections of text documents.

Sentiment classification methods are usually divided into two main categories: Lexicon based techniques and methods based on machine learning. In lexicon-based methods, a rich lexicon of polarized words is used to find key sentences and phrases in text documents which can be used to describe sentiment of the whole text (Taboada et al., 2011). Machine learning methods, on the other hand, treat the sentiment detection problem as a text classification task (Pang et al., 2002).

Most of the research has been oriented towards finding the overall polarity of whole documents. The problem was broken down even more by using of the faceted opinion concept (Liu, 2010). The goal of this attempt was to determine precisely what aspects of the concepts the expressed opinions should be linked to. We will use this distinction to assess our method's viability in both overall and multi faceted opinion analysis.

The work in (Brew et al., 2010) is an attempt to use crowd-sourcing for sentiment analysis. The authors use a crowd of volunteers for the analysis of sentiments of economical news items. Users provide annotations which are then used to learn a classifier to discriminate positive articles from negatives. It uses active learning to select a diverse set of articles for annotations so that a generalizable, precise classifier can be learned from annotated data. The work in (Zhou et al., 2010) is another approach to use active learning to improve sentiment classification. It uses a deep network to learn a sentiment classifier in a semi-supervised manner. Moreover, this method uses active learning to learn from unlabeled data which are the most informative samples that need to be labeled.

Two more recent works that have focused on sentiment classification by designing human computation games are (Weichselbraun et al., 2011) and (Al-Subaihin et al., 2011). In (Weichselbraun et al., 2011) the game "Sentiment Quiz" has been proposed that aims at finding the degree of polarity of words in a lexicon. In each round of the game, the player is asked to vote about polarity of a given words from most negative to most positive. The player is score based on the agreement between his vote and the votes of previous players. "Sentiment Quiz" demands annotation in the word level and therefore can only be used to construct a sentiment lexicon.

Another work which aims at sentiment classification is (Al-Subaihin et al., 2011). In this work, a multi-player game is proposed which aims at finding the sentiment of individual sentences. The game is played by three groups of two players each. Each team is shown a sentence and its members are asked to highlight the sentiment carrying terms of the sentence separately and quickly. The first team whose players' votes match wins and the current game round finishes. The game continues by introducing different sentences to the teams and hence gathers information about polarity of terms and their corresponding context.

3 The Proposed Game

In this section we propose a novel human computation game called Guesstiment. We use the information provided while playing this game to obtain a reliable dataset of sentiment annotated data as well as a lexicon of highly polarized positive and negative words.

Having two by-products as the result of playing instead of merely trying to obtain document annotations is the most important contribution of Guesstiment. The idea of using crowd-sourcing for feature extraction has already been used in (Settles, 2011b), but not as a human computation game. In the rest of the following section, we will discuss the game play and rules of Guesstiment.

3.1 Rules of Guesstiment

Guesstiment is a two-player asynchronous game. It aims at annotating a large corpus of text documents, similar to the goal of the ESP game in (Von Ahn and Dabbish, 2004) for images. However, Guesstiment does this in a different way because of its rules and asynchronous approach. The differences allow Guesstiment to obtain more useful information from played game rounds than ESP does.

The two players of the game are called "Suggester" and "Guesser". These roles are initialized randomly and interchanged between the two players after each round of the game.

The Suggester, who starts each round will be given the whole text of a review document and he/she is supposed to:

1. Decide whether the whole text is positive or negative, i.e. the author is praising about a subject or criticising it.

2. Select a single word (or a sequence of words, as short as possible) which best describes the polarity (positive or negative) he has selected in part (1). For example, when the negative polarity is chosen, the word "terrible" would be a good choice for the representative word (provided that it is present in the text).

The Guesser, on the other hand, will be given only the word (or word sequence) suggested by the Suggester (he won't see the whole text) and he has to guess polarity of the whole text just based on that single word. If the polarities suggested by the two players agree, they are both given some positive score (based on factors described below) otherwise 0. Then the roles are interchanged and the game continues with a new document. The guesser can also refuse to make a guess about polarity of the text (when for example the suggested word is ambiguous or not very discriminative) in which case the suggester has two more opportunities to suggest another word from the text.

Guesstiment is a cooperative game. It means that the two players are not opponent and they both receive equal score after each round (Not high score for one player and low score for the other). Therefore, the Suggester should make his best efforts to select the most polarized word from the test which best describes the selected sentiment or polarity. The UI screens for Suggester and Guesser are depicted in figures 1a and 1b respectively.

3.1.1 Scoring

The score of each suggested word (or word sequence) depends on a variety of factors, including the length of the sequence and its novelty, i.e. how many times it has already been selected by other players. Suppose that the word sequence w is present in the current text document and also it has been present in text documents of n_w of previously played game rounds. Assuming w has been selected k_w time before current game round, the potential score of w, PS_w is defined as:

$$PS_w = \left\lceil \frac{1}{length(w) \times \frac{k_w}{n_w}} \right\rceil \quad (1)$$

In (1), $length(w)$ is the length (number of words) of phrase w. Using this scoring strategy, players are encouraged to select as shortest phrases as possible. Single words that are not already selected by other players will yield the highest score.

Moreover, some words are not allowed as suggestions and will yield zero score regardless of the agreement in polarity judgements. These words are coloured red in the text and are separately displayed in the forbidden list.

The cooperation between the Suggester and the Guesser requires an agreement between them. This allows the game to collect precise annotations and simultaneously build a good quality lexicon of words which are most important in detecting polarity of the text.

The total score of each player is displayed on the scoreboard at the bottom of the Suggest/Guess graphical user interface.

4 Experiments

4.1 Implementation Details

The game was implemented as a traditional three-tier web application. For data storage, we used the H2 embedded database which has proven to be fast enough for scientific information retrieval applications. For the server side of the application we used the Play! framework, which is a lightweight easy to use framework for Java MVC web application framework.

The client side is a Java Applet. We used a service oriented approach to define interactions between the client and the server so that the game play is defined as a sequence of HTTP requests between client and server. Using this approach,, client and server are maximally separate and therefore various client applications can be written, for instance to run on smart phones.

4.2 Experimentation Environment

A total of 80000 review texts were extracted along with their corresponding ratings from the TripAdvisor website [1]. Among these, 1000 articles were randomly selected and inserted in the game database to be used in game rounds. More than 20 players played the game over the course of one month and 697 annotations were collected during this period, of which 312 are distinct.

For selecting articles for each round, a combination of strategies were used. From the set of documents which have not already been labelled by any of the players, we select the article with the least difference between number of positive and negative (as collected in the lexicon constructed so far) words

[1] `http://www.trip-advisor.com`

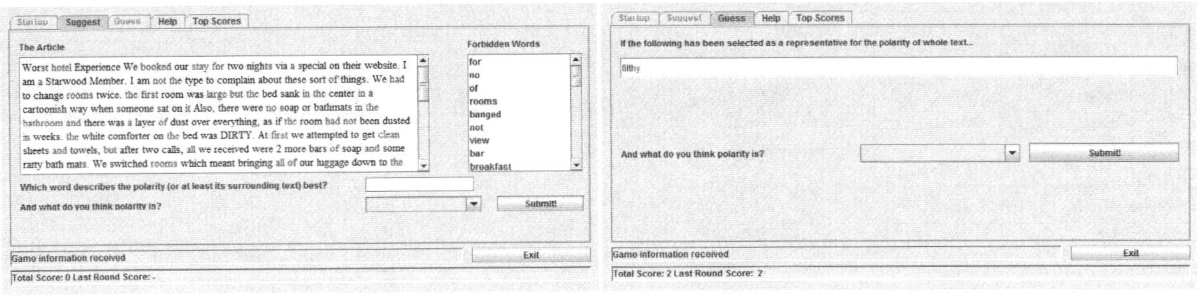

(a) Suggester Role

(b) Guesser Role

Figure 1: The Suggest/Guess UI.

so that we get the most information from annotations. If all document have been annotated at least two times, we make the selection among documents for which the two annotations disagree, so that we solve disagreements by majority vote.

4.3 Quality of Annotations

For each review text in the TripAdvisor website, there is a corresponding rating score given by the very writer of the text. These ratings, score the quality of services of the mentioned hotel from the point of view of the review writer.They give a score of 1 (most negative) to 5 (most positive) to the described hotel which is presumably correlated with the inherent sentiment of the review text written by the same author for the same hotel.

We used these review ratings as the ground truth to assess the quality of player annotations. We considered review ratings higher than 3 as having positive sentiment and those with rating lower than 3 as having negative sentiment. Review with rating equal to 3 were considered neutral and excluded from further experiments. Let $Rate_i$ be the numerical rating of document i, according to the above criteria, we accept document i if and only if:

$$Rate_i \in \{1, 2, 4, 5\} \tag{2}$$

As well as annotations provided by players of the game, we also compared the ground truth to the results of state-of-the-art machine learning techniques adapted for sentiment analysis. We considered sentiment analysis as a typical binary classification problem and used a simple bag of words approach for feature extraction.

For the learning algorithm, we used Support Vector Machines (SVM) and the Naïve Bayes methods which are two well-known learning algorithms for text classification problems (Brew et al., 2010). In the SVM method, document feature vectors are transformed to high-dimensional kernel space and then a maximum margin separating hyperplane is sought in the new kernel space. Training of SVM is quadratic in the amount of training data and therefore it is hardly feasible for large-scale problems.

The Naïve Bayes approach is another learning algorithm which is simpler and faster to run than SVM. In this statistical method, feature words are considered independent random variables and Bayes rule is used to derive posterior probabilities of having positive and negatives sentiment for each document. The sentiment with maximum posterior probability is the predicted sentiment for the given document.

Results of comparison between the ground truth and various annotation approaches are depicted in table 1. For the game results, we aggregated different annotations for individual documents by majority voting. Moreover, for the machine learning algorithms we used cross-validation to adjust the parameters. Moreover, the results were computed by averaging 10-fold cross-validation results over all folds.

Accuracy of each method is defined as:

$$Accuracy = \frac{N_{correct}}{N_{total}} \tag{3}$$

.

In equation (3), $N_{correct}$ is the number of document with computed sentiment equal to the ground

Table 1: Comparison of Game Annotation Accuracies With that of Automatic Classifiers

Method	Accuracy
Game Collected Annotations	**90.4**
Naïve Bayes	80.5
Logistic Regression	83.6
SVM	82.8

truth and N_{total} is the total number of documents. It can be seen in table 1 that our method outperforms machine learning.

4.4 Comparison with Classical Crowd-Sourcing

We also made a comparison between our approach and simple crowd-sourcing. For this goal, we used the results of a survey conducted in summer 2011. 40 of the review texts were selected randomly from the whole dataset and given to a crowd of 27 student to be annotated based on their sentiment. Individual annotations for each document were aggregated using majority voting. The ground truth was computed in the same way as the previous section.

We re-executed the Guesstiment in a period of one week using only those 40 reviews and compared the quality of the obtained annotations to that of the survey (aggregated using majority voting). Similar to the survey, we aggregated annotations for individual documents by majority voting.

The results, depicted in table 2, are quite promising. Accuracy of the simple crowd-sourcing was 82.5% whereas gamification acquired an accuracy of 100%. We can see that merely packaging the problem as a game significantly improves accuracy of the results.

We can infer from tables 1 and 2 that gamification actually helps in obtaining good quality annotation results. Therefore, annotations derived from players' effort are highly reliable and can be used for further studies, discussed below.

4.5 Comparison with Sentiment Dictionary Performance

The previous experiments proved the viability of human computation for detecting the polarities of whole documents. Manual classification is however

Table 2: Comparison between Quality of the Results of Gamification and Crowd-Sourcing

Method	Accuracy
Game Collected Annotations	**100**
Aggregated Crowd Votes	82.5

expensive, even if it takes the form of a game. We take a step further and use the result of the game, in the form of a sentiment dictionary, in a subsequent automated classification task. We compare the Guesstiment dictionary with an established resource, OpinionFinder (Wilson et al., 2005) in a multi faceted opinion classification problem.

The OpinionFinder dictionary (OF) contains 8220 entries representing tuples of English words, either in the original form or stemmed, and their most likely parts of speech. Each tuple has an associated polarity which can be positive, negative or neutral. There are 5276 words in the original form in the dictionary that have a positive or negative polarity. By contrast, the Guesstiment dictionary GS only contains 312 terms, nearly 17 times less than OpinionFinder. Of these, 175 words are negative and 137 positive. Each of the words within the two dictionaries has an intrinsic polarity $P(w), \forall w \in D = \{OF, GS\}$.

The opinion extraction task is topic oriented. We extract faceted opinions (Liu, 2010) - occurrences of sentiment that can be attached to a given topic or class within a topic model $z_i \in \theta, i \in \{1..k\}$ where k is the number of independent topics. We used two sets of topics: the first is a statistical topic model obtained with Latent Dirichlet Allocation (Blei et al., 2003) with $k = 50$ topics from which we retained the most probable 5 words for each topic and created sets of topic relevant terms $\mathcal{P}\{z_i\}$. The second set of topic terms contains the most common 90 nouns in all available hotel reviews, which were afterwards manually separated into 11 classes.

Many Guesstiment dictionary words, such as "value" and "gentleman" bear meaning by themselves (i.e. are nouns) and are not useful in this analysis. However the great majority of the words are adjectives or adverbs. This makes them useful for faceted sentiment analysis. We only consider combinations of topic words and opinion dictionary terms and the allowed combinations are based on grammatical dependency chains:

$$w_1 \xrightarrow{*} w_2, w_1 \in \mathcal{P}\{z_i\}, i = \{1..k\}, w_2 \in D \quad (4)$$

obtained using the Stanford parser (De Marneffe and Manning, 2008).

This binding brings confidence to the model and prevents the accidental misinterpretation of unigrams. Also, the higher granularity of the opinion description allows clustering users based on their preferences.

We define a construct c relevant to a topic z_i within a review r as

$$\begin{gathered} c_{z_i} \in z_i \times D \\ c = (w_1, w_2 | w_1 \in \mathcal{P}\{z_i\}, w_2 \in D, w_1 \xrightarrow{*} w_2) \end{gathered} \quad (5)$$

The polarity of the said relevant construct is given by the orientation of the contained dictionary word:

$$P(c) = P(w_2) \quad (6)$$

The polarity P of the opinion expressed within a review $r \in R$ with respect to a topic z_i is defined as the sum of the polarities of constructs relevant to z_i. This allows us to assess the strength of the opinion expressed with regard to a topic.

$$\begin{gathered} P : R \times \theta \mapsto \mathcal{R} \\ P(r, z_i) = \sum_r P(c_{z_i}), i = \{1..k\} \end{gathered} \quad (7)$$

while the overall polarity of the review is the sum of all topic dependent polarities

$$\begin{gathered} P : R \mapsto \mathcal{R} \\ P(r) = \sum_{i=1}^{k} P(r, z_i) \end{gathered} \quad (8)$$

We test whether the method assigns positive overall polarities to reviews which have high (4 and 5) numeric ratings $nr(r)$ and negative to those with low ones (1 and 2). We compare the precision and recall of the method using both dictionaries and both topic sets. The dataset consists of 2881 reviews regarding the Las Vegas Bellagio hotel. Table 3 summarizes the results. We confine our analysis to a subset of 2594 reviews from the initial 2881 for which the numeric rating is greater or smaller than 3.

We notice that the recall is consistently lower for the frequent noun topics, which was expected because of the significantly smaller number of topic terms. However the recall does not depend on the chosen dictionary. This is relevant because with a much smaller pool of dictionary terms, similar results are obtained. Precision is constant in all four cases, which also shows that results similar to those of OpinionFinder can be obtained with our much smaller dictionary.

The precision and recall values in Table 3 do not reflect the capacity of the higher grained opinion analysis to extract targeted user preferences. The overall variance of the hotel's numeric ratings $Var(nr(r))$ shows how much the reviewers disagree on the quality of the stay. Generally this disagreement comes from the different sets of values the reviewers have. For example some consider cleanliness the most important aspect while others are interested in a busy nightlife.

We cluster users based on the faceted opinions we retrieved, using the k-Means algorithm (MacQueen, 1967). Each reviewer is represented by a feature vector and each feature i within the vector is the cumulative opinion expressed by the reviewer with regard to topic z_i. The reviews within the same cluster j have a similar representation from the mined opinion perspective. If the quality of the opinion mining process is high, the numeric ratings associated to the reviews within a cluster will also be similar, thus their variance $Var_j(nr(r))$ will be lower than the overall variance. We study the difference between the mean intra cluster variance $avgVar_j(nr(r))$ and overall variance $Var(nr(r))$ and the results are shown in table 4 for different numbers of clusters, using both topic models and both dictionaries.

The results show that we succeeded in decreasing the variance by more than 20% using the Guesstiment dictionary and the frequent noun topics. A 17% decrease is obtained by using the same topic set and the OpinionFinder dictionary, while the decreases for the LDA topics with dictionaries are three times lower. This proves that the dictionary resulted from playing the Guesstiment game is better suited for faceted opinion analysis than an established resource like OpinionFinder.

5 Conclusion

In this paper we introduced Guesstiment, a human computation game for simultaneous feature extraction and sentiment annotation. By conducting various experiments, we showed that quality of the annotations obtained using our approach outperforms those obtained by classic crowd-sourcing. This is an indicator of the fact that packaging a crowd-sourcing problem as a game can improve the quality of the obtained results. It's mostly because that games attract more attention from people than simple questions which are common ways of crowd-sourcing.

We also showed that our approach outperforms state-of-the-art machine learning methods which illustrates that human computation power is still superior to machine intelligence in this problem.

The idea of the game could be further extended by testing other more complicated scoring functions which could better motivate players to submit high quality results. Also other document selection strategies can be created to make a better trade-off between informativeness and interestingness, or exploration and exploitation. Moreover, a computer player could be designed to perform active learning on feature extraction and direct the word suggestion process toward selecting more informative features, hereby obtaining a more discriminative high-quality lexicon.

References

A.A. Al-Subaihin, H.S. Al-Khalifa, and A.M.S. Al-Salman. 2011. A proposed sentiment analysis tool for modern arabic using human-based computing. In *Proceedings of the 13th International Conference on Information Integration and Web-based Applications and Services*, pages 543–546. ACM.

David M Blei, Andrew Y Ng, and Michael I Jordan. 2003. Latent dirichlet allocation. *Journal of Machine Learning Research*, 3(4-5):993–1022.

Anthony Brew, Derek Greene, and Padraig Cunningham. 2010. Using crowdsourcing and active learning to track sentiment in online media. In *ECAI*, volume 215 of *Frontiers in Artificial Intelligence and Applications*, pages 145–150. IOS Press.

J. Chamberlain, M. Poesio, and U. Kruschwitz. 2008. Phrase detectives: A web-based collaborative annotation game. *Proceedings of I-Semantics, Graz.*

Emmanuel Christophe, Jordi Inglada, and Jerome Maudlin. 2010. Crowd-sourcing satellite image analysis. In *IGARSS*, pages 1430–1433. IEEE.

Marie-Catherine De Marneffe and Christopher D Manning. 2008. The stanford typed dependencies representation. *Coling 2008 Proceedings of the workshop on CrossFramework and CrossDomain Parser Evaluation CrossParser 08*, 1(ii):1–8.

Andrea Esuli and Fabrizio Sebastiani, 2006. *SentiWordNet: A publicly available lexical resource for opinion mining*, volume 6, page 417422. Citeseer.

C.J. Ho, T.H. Chang, J.C. Lee, J.Y. Hsu, and K.T. Chen. 2009. Kisskissban: a competitive human computation game for image annotation. In *Proceedings of the ACM SIGKDD Workshop on Human Computation*, pages 11–14. ACM.

J. Howe. 2006. The rise of crowdsourcing. *Wired magazine*, 14(14):1–5.

E. Law, B. Settles, A. Snook, H. Surana, L. von Ahn, and T. Mitchell. Human computation for attribute and attribute value acquisition.

Bing Liu. 2010. Sentiment analysis : A multi-faceted problem. *Science*, 25(1):76–80.

J. B. MacQueen. 1967. Some methods for classification and analysis of multivariate observations. In *Proceedings of 5th Berkeley Symposium on Mathematical Statistics and Probability*, pages 281–297.

B. Pang, L. Lee, and S. Vaithyanathan. 2002. Thumbs up?: sentiment classification using machine learning techniques. In *Proceedings of the ACL-02 conference on Empirical methods in natural language processing-Volume 10*, pages 79–86. Association for Computational Linguistics.

A.J. Quinn and B.B. Bederson. 2011. Human computation: a survey and taxonomy of a growing field. In *Proceedings of the 2011 annual conference on Human factors in computing systems*, pages 1403–1412. ACM.

Laurel D. Riek, Maria F. O'Connor, and Peter Robinson. 2011. Guess what? a game for affective annotation of video using crowd sourcing. In Sidney K. D'Mello, Arthur C. Graesser, Björn Schuller, and Jean-Claude Martin, editors, *ACII (1)*, volume 6974 of *Lecture Notes in Computer Science*, pages 277–285. Springer.

Anna Rumshisky. 2011. Crowdsourcing word sense definition. In *Linguistic Annotation Workshop*, pages 74–81. The Association for Computer Linguistics.

B. Settles. 2011a. Closing the loop: Fast, interactive semi-supervised annotation with queries on features and instances. In *Conference on Empirical Methods in*

Table 3: Precision and Recall of Overall Review Polarity Detection

		Total	TP	FP	FN	Precision	Recall
LDA	**GS**	2594	1399	456	739	0.75	0.65
	OF	2594	1434	461	699	0.75	0.67
Top Frequency	**GS**	2594	1275	405	914	0.75	0.58
	OF	2594	1362	371	861	0.78	0.61

Table 4: Weighted Average of Intra Cluster Variances

k			**1**	**10**	**11**	**12**	**13**	**14**	**15**	**% Decrease**
Variance	**LDA**	GS	1.03	1.01	0.99	0.99	0.98	0.96	1.01	6.79
		OF	1.03	0.99	0.95	0.99	0.99	1.01	0.96	7.761
	Top Frequency	GS	0.62	0.52	0.52	0.51	0.49	0.52	0.5	20.964
		OF	0.68	0.57	0.59	0.56	0.57	0.56	0.56	17.64

Natural Language Processing (EMNLP), Edinburgh, Scotland, July.

B. Settles. 2011b. Closing the loop: Fast, interactive semi-supervised annotation with queries on features and instances. *Conference on Empirical Methods in Natural Language Processing (EMNLP), Edinburgh, Scotland, July.*

Maite Taboada, Julian Brooke, Milan Tofiloski, Kimberly D. Voll, and Manfred Stede. 2011. Lexicon-based methods for sentiment analysis. *Computational Linguistics*, 37(2):267–307.

Peter D. Turney. 2002. Thumbs up or thumbs down?: semantic orientation applied to unsupervised classification of reviews. In *Proceedings of the 40th Annual Meeting on Association for Computational Linguistics*, ACL '02, pages 417–424, Stroudsburg, PA, USA. Association for Computational Linguistics.

L. Von Ahn and L. Dabbish. 2004. Labeling images with a computer game. In *Proceedings of the SIGCHI conference on Human factors in computing systems*, pages 319–326. ACM.

L. Von Ahn, M. Kedia, and M. Blum. 2006a. Verbosity: a game for collecting common-sense facts. In *Proceedings of the SIGCHI conference on Human Factors in computing systems*, pages 75–78. ACM.

L. Von Ahn, R. Liu, and M. Blum. 2006b. Peekaboom: a game for locating objects in images. In *Proceedings of the SIGCHI conference on Human Factors in computing systems*, pages 55–64. ACM.

L. Von Ahn. 2006. Games with a purpose. *Computer*, 39(6):92–94.

Carl Vondrick, Deva Ramanan, and Donald Patterson. 2010. Efficiently scaling up video annotation with crowdsourced marketplaces. In Kostas Daniilidis, Petros Maragos, and Nikos Paragios, editors, *ECCV (4)*, volume 6314 of *Lecture Notes in Computer Science*, pages 610–623. Springer.

Albert Weichselbraun, Stefan Gindl, and Arno Scharl. 2011. Using games with a purpose and bootstrapping to create domain-specific sentiment lexicons. In Craig Macdonald, Iadh Ounis, and Ian Ruthven, editors, *CIKM*, pages 1053–1060. ACM.

Theresa Wilson, Paul Hoffmann, Swapna Somasundaran, Jason Kessler, Janyce Wiebe, Yejin Choi, Claire Cardie, Ellen Riloff, and Siddharth Patwardhan. 2005. Opinionfinder : A system for subjectivity analysis. *Learning*, (October):34–35.

Shusen Zhou, Qingcai Chen, and Xiaolong Wang. 2010. Active deep networks for semi-supervised sentiment classification. In Chu-Ren Huang and Dan Jurafsky, editors, *COLING (Posters)*, pages 1515–1523. Chinese Information Processing Society of China.

A Serious Game for Building a Portuguese Lexical-Semantic Network

Mathieu Mangeot♠ **Carlos Ramisch**♠♣
♠ GETALP — LIG, University of Grenoble (France)
♣ Federal University of Rio Grande do Sul (Brazil)
FirstName.LastName@imag.fr

Abstract

This paper presents a game with a purpose for the construction of a Portuguese lexical-semantic network. The network creation is implicit, as players collaboratively create links between words while they have fun. We describe the principles and implementation of the platform. As this is an ongoing project, we discuss challenges and long-term goals.We present the current network in terms a quantitative and qualitative analysis, comparing it to other resources. Finally, we describe our target applications.

1 Introduction

The creation of lexical resources like wordnets is time consuming and very costly in terms of manpower. Funding agencies and publishing houses are very reluctant to launch new projects. Ironically, in our globalized nowadays world, the need of such resources for communication is growing. In this context, there is hope for building resources via communities of voluntary contributors. But is it possible to use the Wikipedia paradigm for building a rich and broad-coverage lexical resource reusable by humans and machines in NLP projects? Wordnets are very interesting resources, but they suffer of several limitations. First, even if the English wordnet (Miller et al., 1990) is open source and freely available, this is not the case of the EuroWordnets. Second, wordnets and other manually built thesauri are based on linguists' intuition. Information about up-to-date entities (Facebook, Costa Concordia, etc.) and real-world facts are missing. Third, relations between the synsets of wordnets are of limited semantic kinds. We would like to build other relations at the syntactic and lexical level (e.g. collocations).

Our first goal is to build a rich lexical network for the Portuguese language. The relations between nodes (words) is represented in a sophisticated way, by using lexical-semantical functions à la Mel'čuk (Mel'čuk, 1995) such as the Magn function representing the notion of intensifier: Magn(smoker) = heavy, Magn(bachelor) = confirmed. The resulting network represents the usage of the language, not the norm. Thus, it may contain frequent spelling mistakes or neologisms. This resource is open-source and freely available. It can be used in several applications: lexicography, printed dictionary, text generation, semantic information extraction, ontology learning, etc. The construction of the resource is done indirectly by contributors through a game.

In the next section, the concept of using serious games for building NLP resources will be explained (§ 2). The following section will detail the construction of the Portuguese version of the game (§ 3). Afterwards, we will discuss some preliminary results (§ 4) and finally we present future work (§ 5).

2 Serious Games and NLP

The concept of human contribution, collaboration and computation has been utilized in many applications and scenarios. The work of Luis von Ahn made a breakthrough, especially in ESP game (von Ahn, 2006; von Ahn and Dabbish, 2008). Human computation (crowdsourcing, volunteer contribution) is now seriously considered to be able to solve large computational problems (Speer, 2007). The idea of collecting massive contributions from volunteers through an online game took off recently. Nowadays, many serious games or GWAP "Game With A Purpose" (von Ahn and Dabbish, 2008) projects exist in different domains, like Open Mind Common Sense (Singh et al., 2002), ESP games, Learner (Chklovski and Gil, 2005), or CYC project [1]. Concerning more specifically lexical networks, similar projects exist like "small world of words"[2] launched in 2003 by KU Leuwen. For the moment, this project is limited to building relations of only one kind: associated ideas.

Looking at the Wikipedia project, the idea of building lexical resources with the help voluntary contributors comes to mind. Unfortunately, the Wikipedia paradigm cannot be easily applied to build a dictionary with rich lexical information. In Wikipedia, articles do not need to follow the same structure, while in a dictionary, the same structure and linguistic theory must be applied to all the articles. Moreover, while it is easy to contribute to an encyclopedia entry, not everyone has the linguistic knowledge to contribute to a dictionary. On reading Wiktionary entries, one realizes that the quality cannot be compared to existing paper dictionaries.

When looking at people playing online games through the Internet, one could think that it would be interesting to use this time for playing a game that would build lexical data in the background, specifically data that is difficult to find in existing dictionaries. In this context, the idea of a serious lexical game emerged. The first version was launched for French in 2007 (Lafourcade and Joubert, 2008), which has now around 250,000 nodes and 1,330,000 relations.

Our game aims at building a rich and evolving lexical network comparable to the famous English wordnet (Miller et al., 1990). The principle is as follows: a player *A* initiates a game, an instruction is displayed concerning a type of competency corresponding to a lexical relation (e.g. synonym, antonym, domain, intensifier) and a word *W* is chosen randomly in the database. Player *A* has then a limited amount of time for giving propositions that answer the instruction applied to the word *W*.

The same word *W* with the same instruction is proposed to another player *B* and the process is the same. The two half-games of player *A* and player *B* are asynchronous. For each common answer in *A* and *B*'s propositions, the two players earn a certain amount of points and credits. For the word *W*, the common answers of *A* and *B* players are entered into the database. This process participates in the construction of a lexical network linking terms with typed and weighted relations, validated by pairs of players. The relations are typed by the instructions given to the players and weighted with the number of pair players that proposed them. A more detailed description of the game in French is provided by Lafourcade and Zampa (2009).

3 Portuguese Version

The game interface was translated by a native Portuguese speaker. A preliminary step was to internationalize the text messages by separating them from the interface and storing them in an array, allowing for easy translation in any other language. Simultaneously, we developed, and tested an easy step-by-step installer which makes the deployment of the game as easy as installing a content management system software on a server.

A list of seed words must be provided from which the game will chose the proposed terms at the beginning. As the game evolves, people suggest new words not necessarily in the initial dictionary, thus helping the vocabulary to grow. Two resources were used to compose this list of seed words. The first is the DELAS–PB dictionary from NILC (Muniz, 2004). All nouns, verbs, adjectives and adverbs were extracted, resulting in 67,062 words. As these include a large number of rare words, pilot tests showed that the game became annoying when the player ignored the meaning of most of the proposed words. Therefore, the number of Google hits for every word was obtained and only the 20% most common ones were kept, resulting in a list of 13,413 words. To this, the entries of the Brazilian Open Mind Common Sense network (Anacleto et al., 2008) were added, in order to allow future comparison with this resource. Apertium's lt-toolbox[3] was used in order to obtain the most frequent POS tag for each entry, resulting in 5,129 nouns, 3,672 verbs, 1,176 adjectives, and 201 adverbs. The union with the preceding dictionary resulted in a final seed

[1] `http://game.cyc.com/`

[2] `http://www.smallworldofwords.com/`

[3] `http://wiki.apertium.org/wiki/Lttoolbox`

list of 20,854 words.

Once the game is deployed, one of the big challenges is to gather volunteer players. We gave presentations about the game in the academic context and spread the word among Portuguese teachers, arguing that the game could be used to enrich the vocabulary of their students. We also created a Facebook page and linked it in our website. One way to motivate subscribed players to come back is to offer gift words. Each player can offer a friend a game with a specific word. For example, if I have a friend fan of baseball, I will offer him/her this word.

Once the first challenge of gathering a community of players is overcome, the main difficulty is to keep the motivation going. For succeeding, the project needs a person that will animate the community, motivate gamers and publicize the game for recruiting new contributors. Games were launched in other languages, but due to social factors (lack of community animator), they are in a sleeping state.[4]

Internally, each word is represented as a node in a graph. The directed edges are the lexico-syntactic relations created by the game. Each edge has a type (associated idea, hypernym, hyponym, typical object, etc.) and a weight, corresponding to the number of times the two words co-occurred. Each node has also a weight corresponding to its popularity (proportional to its degree). Part of speech is encoded as edges going from a term to special POS nodes. In addition to the standard attributes, each edge also contains counters that represent the country of players who contributed to its creation. Therefore, we would like to investigate dialectal variations of Portuguese in Portugal, Brasil and other lusophone countries. This information can be important for using the resource in semantic extraction, according to the variation of the analyzed text.

4 Preliminary Evaluation

To date, 61 players participated in the game. In this preliminary quantitative and qualitative evaluation, we consider only the nodes for which some relation was created, thus excluding all the seed words that were not connected to other words yet. Figure 1 shows a fragment of the network. Green edges represent associated words, red edges represent hypo-

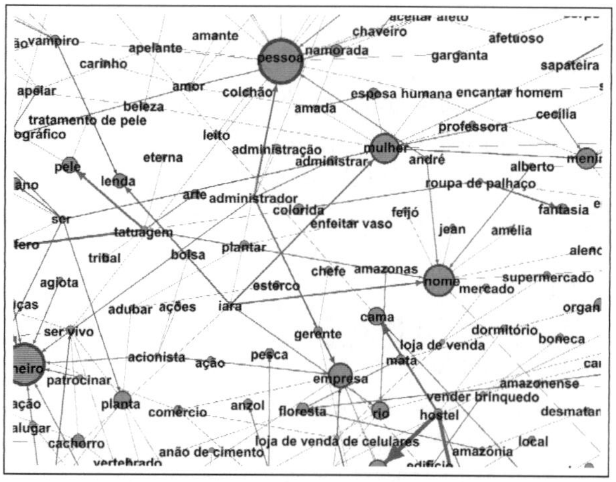

Figure 1: Overview of part of the network.

and hypernyms. Most relations created are standard, like *feijó*, *andré*, *amélia* and *jean* are associated with *name*. However, non-standard relations are also created, like *Cuba* is the antonym of *United States* or *tatoo* is associated to *eternal*. While purists may consider these as noise, we regard it as relations representing real-world semantics and language use.

The network contains 19,473 word nodes and 20,854 occurrences of POS relations (a word may have several POS). Among those, 347 nodes do not contain POS edges, meaning that they are new words. A sample of the 20 most popular terms is presented in Table 1. They include common hypernym nodes like *thing* and *person* and *animal* but also everyday language words like *drink*, *car* and *sea*.

From all the nodes in the network, only 1,408 (7.23%) have a degree greater than 1 (excluding POS edges). For the remaining 18,065 nodes, no relation was created. Figure 2 shows user activity in number of games played per day. The number of games is unsteady but it does not seem to increase nor decrease. Analysis of the log files show that players tend to participate a lot and the beginning and then, after one or two weeks, they stop. Thus, it is important not only to attract new players but also to keep them active.

Word	w	Word	w	Word	w
comida	110	hotel	80	pintura	74
***	100	bebida	80	água	72
pessoa	96	mulher	78	porta	72
dinheiro	92	casa	78	mar	72
carne	82	carro	78	empresa	72
nome	80	animal	76	coisa	72

Table 1: Top-20 most connected words and weights (w).

[4] http://jeuxdemots.liglab.fr/

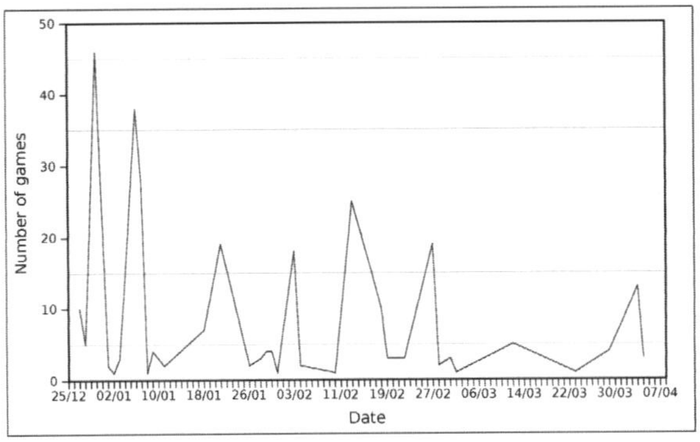

Figure 2: User activity from Dec 27, 2011 to Apr 4, 2012.

For the moment, the most common edge is of the associated idea type. It corresponds to more than 80% of the edges. Some players bought competences in hypo- and hypernym, which together account for 15.39% of the edges. As these relations are dual, it would be easy to infer new edges.The total number of edges acquired is 1,344.

There is one large connected component in the graph and a large number of small connected components with two or three nodes. The total number of connected components in the graph is 281 (ignoring disconnected nodes), yielding a high modularity of 0.898. The average degree of a node is 0.955, as more than 750 nodes have only one relation and around 200 have 2 relations, and the degree decreases exponentially.

The trend is that, as more relations are added, the current small components will be attached to the larger ones, but also more smaller unconnected graphs will be created. However, we expect that once a large proportion of the nodes has been covered, the network will converge to a single large connected component.

For the moment, the coverage of our resource is limited. But a previous comparison done for the French game versus the French Euro WordNet (F-EWN) was very promising. The french game contains 10 times more terms than F-EWN (240,000 vs 23,000) and relations (1,359,000 vs 100,000). On a sample of 100 terms frequently played in the game, 3% of them contain errors (spelling mistakes or confusions). Data collected with the French game bring a lot of originality but the precision rate is much lower that data collected manually in F-EWN.

Relation type	Count	%
Associated	1,126	83.78
Hypernym	115	8.56
Hyponym	81	6.83
Domain	12	0.89
Antonym	10	0.74
Total	1,344	100

Table 2: Number of edges according to types.

Our resource now only contains as much as 0.91% of the nodes in English Wordnet. As precise numbers about the size of the Portuguese wordnet (Marrafa et al., 2011) are not available, we also queried the online service for the nodes in our network. We found out that 35.87% of the nodes are covered by the Portuguese wordnet. Thus, we believe that collaborative methods can considerably speed up the creation of lexical resources, as in only three months we already have some information complimentary to a 13-years old project.

5 Future work

We presented the deployment and a preliminary evaluation of JeuxDeMots–pt,[5] a game that aims at the construction of a Portuguese lexical-semantic network. The coverage of the resource is still limited, but the network keeps growing.

For the moment, we have made available a simple interface in which the user can query for a word and retrieve all the words related to it. For instance, if one searches for the word *loja (store)*, the result is:

- *store* is a *place*
- *cell phone store* is a *store*
- *store* is associated to *buy shirt*
- *store* is associated to *sell toys*
- *store* is associated to *manager*
- *store* is associated to *clothes*

The creation of the network is much less onerous and faster (and more entertaining) than traditional thesauri construction, that can take years of the work of many experts. Our long-term goal is the creation of a large network comparable to existing resources for English. This resource would be extremely useful in many NLP tasks. Once we will have enough data, our goal is to apply it to many other applications like information extraction, WSD, semantic inference and textual entailment. This would help to bridge the gap of missing lexical resources for NLP applications dealing with Portuguese language.

[5] `http://jeuxdemots.liglab.fr/por`

Acknowledgements

This work was partly funded by the CAMELEON project (CAPES–COFECUB 707-11).

References

Junia Coutinho Anacleto, Aparecido Fabiano P. de Carvalho, Alexandre M. Ferreira, Eliane N. Pereira, and Alessandro J. F. Carlos. 2008. Common sense based applications to advance personalized learning. In *PROC of the IEEE International Conference on Systems, Man and Cybernetics (SMC 2008)*, pages 3244–3249, Singapore.

Timothy Chklovski and Yolanda Gil. 2005. An analysis of knowledge collected from volunteer contributors. In *Twentieth National Conference on Artificial Intelligence (AAAI-05)*, Pittsburgh, Pennsylvania.

Mathieu Lafourcade and Alain Joubert. 2008. Jeuxdemots : un prototype ludique pour l'émergence de relations entre termes. In *JADT 2008 : 9es Journées internationales d'Analyse statistique des Données Textuelles*, pages 657–666, Lyon, France, 12-14 mars.

Mathieu Lafourcade and Virginie Zampa. 2009. Jeuxdemots and pticlic: games for vocabulary assessment and lexical acquisition. In *Computer Games, Multimedia & Allied technology 09 (CGAT'09)*, Singapore, 11th-13th May.

Palmira Marrafa, Raquel Amaro, and Sara Mendes. 2011. Wordnet.pt global – extending wordnet.pt to portuguese varieties. In *Proc. of the First Workshop on Algorithms and Resources for Modelling of Dialects and Language Varieties*, pages 70–74, Edinburgh, Scotland, July. ACL.

Igor Mel'čuk. 1995. Lexical functions: A tool for the description of lexical relations in the lexicon. In Leo Wanner, editor, *Lexical Functions in Lexicography and Natural Language Processing*, pages 37–102. John Benjamins, Amsterdam/Philadelphia.

George A. Miller, Richard Beckwith, Christiane Fellbaum, Derek Gross, and Katherine Miller. 1990. Introduction to wordnet: an on-line lexical database. *International Journal of Lexicography*, 3(4):235–244.

Marcelo C. M. Muniz. 2004. A construção de recursos linguistico-computacionais para o portugues do brasil: o projeto de unitex-pb. Master's thesis, Instituto de Ciencias Matematicas de Sao Carlos, USP, São Carlos, SP, Brazil.

Push Singh, Thomas Lin, et al. 2002. Open mind common sense: Knowledge acquisition from the general public. In *Proceedings of the First International Conference on Ontologies, Databases, and Applications of Semantics for Large Scale Information Systems*, Irvine, CA, USA.

Robert Speer. 2007. Open mind commons: An inquisitive approach to learning common sense. In *Workshop on Common Sense and Intelligent User Interfaces*, Honolulu, Hawaii, USA., January 28-31.

Luis von Ahn and Laura Dabbish. 2008. General techniques for designing games with a purpose. *Communications of the ACM*, pages 58–67.

Luis von Ahn. 2006. Games with a purpose. *IEEE Computer Magazine*, pages 96–98.

Collaboratively Building Language Resources while Localising the Web

Asanka Wasala, Reinhard Schäler, Ruvan Weerasinghe* and Chris Exton
Centre for Next Generation Localisation/Localisation Research Centre
CSIS Department, University of Limerick, Limerick, Ireland
*University of Colombo School of Computing, 35, Reid Avenue, Colombo 00700, Sri Lanka
{Asanka.Wasala, Reinhard.Schaler, Chris.Exton}@ul.ie,
*arw@ucsc.cmb.ac.lk

Abstract

In this paper, we propose the collaborative construction of language resources (translation memories) using a novel browser extension-based client-server architecture that allows translation (or 'localisation') of web content capturing and aligning source and target content produced by the 'power of the crowd'. The architectural approach chosen enables collaborative, in-context, and real-time localisation of web content supported by the crowd and high-quality language resources. To the best of our knowledge, this is the only practical web content localisation methodology currently being proposed that incorporates the collaborative construction and use of TMs. The approach also supports the building of resources such as parallel corpora – resources that are still not available for many, and especially not for underserved languages.

1 Introduction

A vast amount of knowledge is available on the web, primarily in English. There are millions of people worldwide, who cannot assimilate this knowledge mainly due the language service barrier. Although English is still dominating the web, the situation is changing. Non-English content is growing rapidly (Large and Moukdad, 2000; Daniel Brandon, 2001; Wasala and Weerasinghe, 2008).

Localisation is the translation and adaptation of digital content. Localisation of a website involves "translating text, content and adjusting graphical and visual elements, content and examples to make them culturally appropriate" (Stengers et al., 2004). However, the scope of our research is limited to the translation of text, which is arguably the most crucial component of web content localisation.

The study of web content localisation is a relatively new field within academia (Jiménez-Crespo, 2011). The only reported approaches to website localisation are human (Daniel Brandon, 2001) and machine-based translation (Large and Moukdad, 2000; Daniel Brandon, 2001; Wasala and Weerasinghe, 2008), with only very basic collaborative (Horvat, 2012) or first in-context approaches (Boxma, 2012) attempted. Although researchers have reported on the use of Machine Translation (MT) in web content localisation (Gaspari, 2007), the low quality of the MT-based website translation solutions is known to have been a significant drawback (Large and Moukdad, 2000; Daniel Brandon, 2001). Moreover, the research and development of MT systems for less-resourced languages is still in its infancy (Wasala and Weerasinghe, 2008). Therefore, MT-based web content localisation solutions are clearly not viable for less-resourced languages.

Undoubtedly, Web 2.0 and the constant increase of User Generated Content (UGC) lead to a higher demand for translation. The trend of crowdsourcing/social translation came into play only in the last few years. In this paper, we focus on crowdsourcing translation, i.e. when the crowd or a motivated part of it, participates in an open call to translate some content, creating highly valuable language resources in the process.

Browser extensions enhance the functionality of web browsers. Various browser extensions already exist that are capable of utilising existing Machine Translation (MT) services to translate web content into different languages. We exploit the power of browser extensions to design a conceptual localization layer for the web. Our research is mainly inspired by the works of Exton et al. (2009) on real-time localisation of desktop software using the crowd, Wasala and Weerasngihe (2008) on browser based pop-up dictionary extension, and Schäler on information sharing across languages (2012a) as well as social localisation (2012b).

The proposed architecture enables in-context real-time localisation of web content by communities sharing not just their content but also their language skills. The ultimate aim of this work is the collaborative creation of TMs which will allow for the automatic translation of web content based on reviewed and quality-checked, human produced translations. To the best of the authors' knowledge, this is the first effort of its kind to utilise the power of browser extensions along with TMs to build a website independent conceptual localisation layer with the aid of crowdsourcing.

The rest of the paper is organized as follows: Section 2 describes the architecture of the proposed system in detail; the development of the prototype is discussed in section 3; section 4 discusses key outstanding challenges and constraints of the proposed architecture; and finally, this paper concludes with a summary and discussion of future research directions.

2 System Architecture

In this section, the main functionalities of the proposed system architecture are described in detail.

The proposed system architecture is based on earlier work by Exton et al. (2009). They proposed a client-server architecture known as Update-Log-Daemon (UpLoD) for the localisation of applications' User Interface (UI) by the crowd. However, in our architecture, clients (browsers) connect to the central server via a browser extension. The browser extension implements the UpLoD architecture, which acts as a proxy between the browser and the central server.

We also extend the functionality of the central server in this architecture by equipping it with a component to maintain TMs for different language pairs.

2.1 Content Retrieval and Rendering Process

When the browser extension is installed and enabled, it allows a user to select the preferred locale. When a new URL is typed in, the browser will download the page. As soon as the content is downloaded, the browser extension will consult the central server for any TM matches in the user's preferred locale for the relevant URL. The TM matches will be retrieved with the contextual information. The next step is to replace the original content with the retrieved TM matches. With the aid of contextual hints that it received, the TM matches (i.e. target strings) will be replaced with the source strings. Finally, the content will be rendered in the browser. The contextual information may include: URL, last update date/time stamp, surrounding text with and without tags, XPath location of the segment, CSS properties among others as this information will helpful to precisely locate HTML elements in a web page (Selenium 2012). For replacing the original text with target strings, techniques such as Regular-expressions matching and XPath queries may be utilized.

2.2 Content Translation Process

The browser extension also facilitates the in-context translation of source content. Right clicking on a selected text will bring up a contextual menu where a "Translate" sub-menu can be found.

The extension allows in-context translation of the selected content segment in an editing environment similar to Wikipedia. Once the translation is completed, the extension sends the translated segment, original content and contextual information including URL to the central sever. Upon receiving translations from a client, the central server stores all the information that it retrieves in a TM.

The central server can be scheduled to periodically leverage translations as the TMs grow. Furthermore, later on, MT systems can be trained from the TM data and these trained MT systems can feed back into the system to speed up the translation process as well as to translate the content where TM matches are not found.

2.3 Translation Editing and Voting Process

As in the case of software localisation (Exton et al., 2009), a mechanism has to be built to choose the most appropriate translation of a given text segment. To assist in selecting the best translation for a given segment, a voting mechanism is proposed.

However, human intervention (mainly the opinions of experts) is essential to solve potential conflicts.

Right clicking on a translated segment brings up a context menu, where the current translation along with the top 3 alternative translations is displayed. The votes for each translation will also be displayed next to the translation. The users are given the opportunity to edit the current translation and/or to vote any of the alternative translations.

Furthermore, clicking on an alternative translation will take the user to a web page where the user can see all the alternative translations that are proposed for the selected segment. In that page users can vote for any of the alternate translations.

Considering the motivation factors related to crowdsourcing, a simple "thumbs up, thumbs down" voting is proposed over complex and confusing rating systems. If the user wishes to edit the existing translation, they can simply go to the in-context edit mode and edit the content. Once editing has been performed, the new translation is sent back to the central server. The central server compares the new changes with the existing translations and includes it as an alternative translation.

The central server needs to keep track of the votes as well as the voters. By keeping track of voters, users can be encouraged to vote for additional translations using ranking systems similar to those implemented in games.

3 Development of the Prototype

To test the above architecture, we developed a prototype with the aid of two open source Firefox Add-ons:

1. *Ingiya* – a pop-up dictionary Firefox add-on similar to the add-on described by Wasala and Weerasinghe (2008);
2. *FoxReplace* – a Firefox add-on that can automatically replace textual content with the aid of a predefined substitution list.

Ingiya, a non-intrusive add-on, shows Sinhala definitions of English terms when the mouse pointer is hovered on top of English words in a web site. It is also capable of temporarily replacing Sinhala definitions with English words (i.e. as soon as the page is refreshed, the translations disappear). Currently, the Ingiya add-on only supports individual words. The dictionary entries are stored within a local database.

The add-on was first modified to support phrases (selected text segments) in addition to individual words and to be able to collect translations for a selected phrase from the user. We submitted the selected text segment, user's translations and the URL of the active tab of the browser via Ingiya add-on to the central server as a RESTful call. We encoded the above data using the *Punycode* algorithm prior to submission.

We then implemented the central server using PHP. In this prototype, the server mainly performs three functions: 1) It accepts data sent via browser add-ons, decode the data and stores in it's local database 2) Upon a request from a client, it transforms and sends the data in its local database into a XML based format understood by FoxReplace addon, 3) It can transform and sends data in it's local database into an XML Localisation Interchange File Format (XLIFF) file that can be used as a TM.

The FoxReplace add-on is capable of retrieving a regular expression-based source and target substitution list encoded in a specific XML format and replacing text in a web page. Different substitutions can be defined for different URLs. The FoxReplace add-on was configured to retrieve translations (i.e. substitution list) from the central server. When combined, these two add-ons along with the central server are able to implement and demonstrate the UpLoD architecture described in the pervious section. The exception is the voting mechanism which has not yet been implemented but is part of on-going work by the research group.

4 Discussion: Outstanding Challenges

While most of the issues and challenges emphasised in the UpLoD-based architecture (Exton et al., 2009) are common to the architecture proposed in this article, web content localisation also faces additional, unique technical challenges.

Web pages consist of not only text, but also non-textual content such as images, audio clips, videos and various embedded objects (e.g. Java, Flash, PDF or Silverlight content) (Daniel Brandon 2001; Stengers et al., 2004). Textual content represented in graphics such as banners is also very common in web sites. The current architecture however does not deal with localisation of non-textual content found in websites. Even with the textual content, font and rendering problems may surface in the localised version.

Another issue that can occur in a crowdsourced localisation model as noted by Exton et al. (2009) is the primary focus on translation of the frequently used content by the crowd. This issue is likely to surface in the web content localisation scenario as well. It will result in untranslated content of infrequently visited sections of the web sites.

Issues related to translation voting, especially the 'thrashing' scenarios as described by Exton et al. (2009) need to be addressed in this scenario too. The optimum human translation rating mechanisms, as well as motivations for rating these, have to be explored further.

Another important factor is the design of a methodology for coping with constant updates of websites. We would expect that a large TM might help to alleviate the above problem to a certain degree.

One of the advantages of the above methodology is that, once the entire web page is completely translated, the translated page can be cached in the central server for improved performance. On the other hand, the localisation layer is only accessible via the browser extension. Therefore, users are not able to interact with the website using their native language, nor would these pages be indexed by search engines (i.e. the localised version).

In addition to various technical issues discussed above, legal issues could potentially be encountered which need to be thoroughly examined, identified and addressed prior to the deployment of the proposed solution. The first question that needs to be answered is if people have a right to localise websites without the consent of the web site owners. Moreover, the TMs (for each language pair) will keep on growing once the crowd starts using this framework. Legal implications around the TMs have to be thoroughly considered. For example, questions such as who owns the TMs needs to be addressed.

The accuracy of the translations is one of the crucial aspects that need to be considered. It is essential to investigate necessary steps to prevent possible misuse. Misuse of the service can be alleviated to a certain extent by developing a log-on mechanism where users have to be authenticated by the central server to access the localisation service. Furthermore, individuals who contribute translations as well as individuals who vote for translations can be tracked and rewarded. Thus, these individuals can be further motivated with the use of public announcements and ranking (or medal offering) systems as in games.

Website localisation is not just the translation of text in a website. Various ethical, cultural and regional issues have to be taken into account when localising a website. Therefore, a reviewing mechanism such as observed in the Wikipedia community has to be built in to this model.

5 Conclusions and Future Work

In this paper, we have discussed the development of a browser extension-based website independent client-server architecture that facilitates the collaborative creation of TMs used for the localisation of web content. As this approach uses TMs constructed with the aid of the crowd and reviewed by experts where necessary, rather than an MT system, better quality translations can be expected. The development of the prototype has proven the viability of the proposed approach. Future research will focus mainly on addressing the issues related to central server services discussed above. Moreover, the development of a (single) Firefox add-on encompassing all the functionalities described in section 3 has already shown good results.

To the best of our knowledge, this is the only practical web content localisation approach proposed which is based on the collaborative construction of TMs utilising the power of browser extensions combined with micro-crowdsourcing. The current architecture will be especially useful in the case of less-resourced languages where MT systems are not (yet) viable. The proposed system focuses on the building of language resources, such as translation memories but also parallel corpora, which could be used for the development of MT systems in the future.

Acknowledgments

This research is supported by the Science Foundation Ireland (Grant 07/CE/I1142) as part of the Centre for Next Generation Localisation at the University of Limerick. The prototype was implemented based on Ingiya and FoxReplace add-ons. The authors would like to thank the authors of and the contributors to the above add-ons.

References

Boxma, H. (2012). RIGI Localization Solutions Retrieved April 01, 2012, from https://sites.google.com/a/rigi-ls.com/www/home

Daniel Brandon, J. (2001). Localization of web content. *J. Comput. Small Coll., 17*(2), 345-358.

Exton, C., Wasala, A., Buckley, J., & Schäler, R. (2009). Micro Crowdsourcing: A new Model for Software Localisation. *Localisation Focus, 8*(1), 81-89.

Gaspari, F. (2007). *The Role of Online MT in Webpage Translation.* Doctor of Philosophy, University of Manchester, Manchester, Retrieved June 28, 2011, from http://www.localisation.ie/resources/Awards/Theses/F_Gaspari_Thesis.pdf

Horvat, M. (2012). *Live Website Localization.* W3C Workshop: The Multilingual Web – The Way Ahead, Luxembourg, Retrieved April 01, 2012, from http://mozeg.com/pontoon-mlw.html

Jiménez-Crespo, M. A. (2011). To adapt or not to adapt in web localization: a contrastive genre-based study of original and localised legal sections in corporate websites. *JoSTrans (The Journal of Special Translation)*(15).

Large, A., & Moukdad, H. (2000). Multilingual access to web resources: an overview. *Program: Electronic Library and Information Systems, 34*(1), 43 - 58. doi: 10.1108/EUM0000000006938

Schäler, R. (2012a). Information Sharing Across Languages Computer-Mediated Communication across Cultures: International Interactions in Online Environments (pp. 215-234): IGI Global.

Schäler, R. (2012b). Introducing *Social Localisation.* Workshop. Localization World, Silicon Valley,. Retrieved April 02, 2012 from http://www.slideshare.net/TheRosettaFound/social-localisation

Selenium Project. (2012). Selenium-IDE - Locating Elements. Retreived May 14, 2012 from: http://seleniumhq.org/docs/02_selenium_ide.html#locating-elements

Stengers, H., Troyer, O. D., Baetens, M., Boers, F., & Mushtaha, A. N. (2004). *Localization of Web Sites: Is there still a need for it?* Paper presented at the International Workshop on Web Engineering (held in conjunction with the ACM HyperText 2004 Conference), Santa Cruz, USA.

Wasala, A., & Weerasinghe, R. (2008). *EnSiTip: A Tool to Unlock the English Web.* Paper presented at the 11th International Conference on Humans and Computers, Nagaoka University of Technology, Japan.

Resolving Task Specification and Path Inconsistency in Taxonomy Construction

Hui Yang
Department of Computer Science
Georgetown University
37th and O street NW
Washington, DC, 20057
huiyang@cs.georgetown.edu

Abstract

Taxonomies, such as Library of Congress Subject Headings and Open Directory Project, are widely used to support browsing-style information access in document collections. We call them browsing taxonomies. Most existing browsing taxonomies are manually constructed thus they could not easily adapt to arbitrary document collections. In this paper, we investigate both automatic and interactive techniques to derive taxonomies from scratch for arbitrary document collections. Particular, we focus on encoding user feedback in taxonomy construction process to handle task-specification rising from a given document collection. We also addresses the problem of path inconsistency due to local relation recognition in existing taxonomy construction algorithms. The user studies strongly suggest that the proposed approach successfully resolve task specification and path inconsistency in taxonomy construction.

1 Introduction

Taxonomies, such as Library of Congress Subject Headings (LCSH, 2011) and Open Directory Project (ODP, 2011), are widely used to support browsing-style information access in document collections. We call them browsing taxonomies. Browsing taxonomies are tree-structured hierarchies built upon a given document collection. Each term in a browsing hierarchy categorizes a set of documents related to this term. Driven by their needs, users can navigate through a the hierarchical structure of a browsing taxonomy to access particular documents. A browsing taxonomy can benefit information access via (1) providing an overview of (important) concepts in a document collection, (2) increasing the visibility of documents ranked low in a list (e.g. documents ordered by search relevance), and (3) presenting together documents about the same concept to allow more focused reading.

Most existing browsing taxonomies are manually constructed thus they could not easily adapt to arbitrary document collections. However, it is not uncommon that document collections are given ad-hoc for specific tasks, such as search result organization in for individual search queries (Carpineto et al., 2009) and literature investigation for a new research topic (Chau et al., 2011). There is a necessity to explore automatic or interactive techniques to support *quick* construction of browsing taxonomies for arbitrary document collections.

Most research on automatic taxonomy construction focuses on identifying local relations between concept pairs (Etzioni et al., 2005; Pantel and Pennacchiotti, 2006). The infamous problem of *path inconsistency*, which are usually caused by the local nature of most relation recognition algorithms when building a taxonomy, commonly exists in current research. Oftentimes, when a connecting concept for two pairs of parent-child concepts has multiple senses or represent mixed perspectives, the problem shows up. For example, while *financial institute→bank* and *bank→river bank* are correct; the path *financial institute→bank→river bank* is semantically inconsistent.

In this paper, we propose a semi-supervised distance learning method to construct task-specific taxonomies. Assuming that a user is present to construct a taxonomy for browsing, the proposed approach directly learns semantic distances from the manual guidance provided by the user to predict semantically meaningful browsing taxonomies. Moreover, We tackle path inconsistency by posing constraints over root-to-leaf paths in a hierarchy to ensure concept consistency within paths

The contributions of our work include:

- It offers an opportunity for handling task specifications.
- Unlike most algorithms, our work takes care of path consistency during taxonomy construction.

The remainder of this paper is organized as follows: Section 2 describes the related work. Section 3 details the proposed automated algorithm for taxonomy construction. Section 4 presents the interactive algorithm to incorporate user feedback under a supervised semantic distance learning framework. Section 5 describes the evaluation and Section 6 concludes the paper.

2 Related Work

Most research conducted in the NLP community focuses on extracting local relations between concept pairs (Hearst, 1992; Berland and Charniak, 1999; Ravichandran and Hovy, 2002; Girju et al., 2003; Etzioni et al., 2005; Pantel and Pennacchiotti, 2006; Kozareva et al., 2008). More recently, more attention has been paid in building full taxonomies. For example, (Kozareva and Hovy, 2010) proposed to connect local concept pairs by finding the longest path in a subsumption graph. Both (Snow et al., 2006) and (Yang and Callan, 2009) incrementally grew taxonomies by adding new concepts at optimal positions within the existing structures. Specifically, Snow et al. estimated conditional probabilities by using syntactic parse features and decided taxonomic structure via maximizing overall likelihood of taxonomy. Yang and Callan proposed the ME framework to model the semantic distance $d(c_x, c_y)$ between concepts c_x and c_y as a weighted combination of numerous lexical and semantic features: $\sum_j \text{weight}_j * \text{feature}_j(c_x, c_y)$ and determine the taxonomic structure by minimizing overall distances.

An advantage in ME is that it allows manipulations to concept positions by incorporating various constraints to taxonomic structures. For example, ME handled concept generality-specificity by learning different distance functions for general concepts (located at upper levels) and specific concepts (located at lower levels) in a taxonomy.

In the Information Retrieval (IR) community, browsing taxonomies. also often called browsing hierarchies or Web directories, has been studied as an alternative to the ranked list representation for search results by the Information Retrieval (IR) community. The proposed forms of browsing structures include topic clusters (Cutting et al., 1992) and monothetic concept hierarchies (Sanderson and Croft, 1999; Lawrie et al., 2001; Kummamuru et al., 2004; Carpineto et al., 2009). The latter uses single concepts to represent documents containing them and organizes the concepts into hierarchies; they are in fact taxonomies. The major drawback of these approaches is that they often fail to produce meaningful taxonomic structures due to neglecting the semantics among concepts. For instance, (Sanderson and Croft, 1999) used document frequency and (Lawrie et al., 2001) used conditional probability to derive *is-a* relations. Moreover, they also suffer from path inconsistency when building full taxonomies.

3 Browsing Taxonomy Construction

To build browsing taxonomy for a document collection, the first step is to extract the concepts. We take a simple but effective approach. We exhaustively examine the collection and output a large set of terms, formed by nouns, noun phrases, and named entities occurring >5 times in the collection. We then filter out invalid terms due to part-of-speech errors or misspelling by removing terms that occur <4 times out of the top 10 returned snippets when submitting the term to *google.com* as a search query. We further conflate similar terms into clusters using LSA (Bellegarda et al., 1996) and select the most frequent terms as concepts from each term group. We select the N most frequent concepts to form the concept set C. N usually ranges from 30 to 100. We assume that C contains all concepts in the browsing taxonomy;

even when an important concept for the collection is missing, we will "make do" with C. This may lead to some errors, but can be later corrected by users through proposing new concepts interactively (Section 4).

This section presents how to automatically build taxonomies. We introduce the semantic distance learning method in Section 3.1 and present how to achieve path consistency control in Section 3.2.

3.1 Semantic Distance Learning

To support browsing in arbitrary collections, in this paper, we propose to incorporate task specification in a taxonomy. One way to achieve it is to define task-specific distances among concepts. Moreover, through controlling distance scores among concepts, we can enforce path consistency in taxonomies. For example, when the distance between *financial institute* and *river bank* is big, the path *financial institute→bank→river bank* will be pruned and the concepts will be repositioned. Inspired by ME, we take a distance learning approach to deal with path consistency (Section 3) and task specification (Section 4) in taxonomy construction. In this section, we demonstrate how to estimate semantic distances from training data.

We assume that there are some underlying feature functions that measure semantic dissimilarity for two concepts from various aspects and a good semantic distance is a combination of all features. Different from ME, we model the semantic distance between concepts (c_x, c_y) as a Mahalanobis distance (Mahalanobis, 1936):

$$d_{c_x,c_y} = \sqrt{\Phi(c_x, c_y)^T W^{-1} \Phi(c_x, x_y)} \quad (1)$$

$d_{c_x,c_y} = \sqrt{\Phi(c_x, c_y)^T W^{-1} \Phi(c_x, x_y)}$, where $\Phi(c_x, c_y)$ represents the set of pairwise underlying feature functions, where each feature function is $\phi_k : (c_x, c_y)$ with k=1,...,$|\Phi|$. W is a weight matrix, whose diagonal values weigh the underlying feature functions. When only diagonal values of W are taken into account, W is equivalent to assigning weights to different axes in the random vectors.

Note that a semantic distance is still a distance metric. One important characteristic of a valid distance metric is that it must represent valid clustering partitions, which means that the clustering partitions represented by the distance metric should be consistent. Therefore, certain constraints need to be satisfied. An obvious one is that concepts in the same cluster should have smaller distance scores than those in different clusters. Moreover, a valid distance metric should be non-negative and satisfy the triangle inequality. To ensure such regularities, we need to constrain W to be positive semi-definite (PSD) (Bhatia, 2006):

$$W \succeq 0.$$

Since we assume that a good semantic distance is a combination of all these features, we can decompose the task of semantic distance learning into two subtasks - identifying good features and learning the weight matrix from training data.

In our approach, we employ a wide range of features to cover various aspects in measuring dissimilarity between concepts. Given two concepts c_x and c_y, a feature is defined as a function $\phi : (c_x, c_y)$ enerating a value within [0,1]. In total, we used 31 features, including *lexical-syntactic patterns, contextual, co-occurrence, syntactic dependency*, and *definitions*.

Similar to the linguistic approaches, we use *lexical-syntactic patterns* to evaluate relations among concepts. Our patterns include hypernym patterns such as "c_x, *and other* c_y", sibling patterns such as "c_x *and* c_y", and part-of patterns such as "c_x *consists of* c_y". Each feature returns a boolean value of wether it can find instances for the pattern in text.

Besides patterns, we used more semantic features. For example, since word meanings can be inferred from and represented by contexts, we develop several *contextual* features. One is *Local Context KL-Divergence*, which measures the Kullback-Leibler divergence between two unigram language models built for c_x and c_y upon all left two and right two words surrounding them. Moreover, we formulate the *co-occurrence* features as point-wise mutual information between (c_x, c_y):

$$pmi(c_x, c_y) = log \frac{Count(c_x, c_y)}{Count(c_x)Count(c_y)},$$

where $Count(.)$ is defined as the number of documents or sentences containing the concept(s), or n as in "Results 1-10 of about n for term" appearing on the first page of Google search results for querying c_x, c_y, or $c_x c_y$.

We also generate *syntactic dependency* features via syntactic parse[1] and semantic role labeling[2]. For example, we measure how many overlaps exist between c_x's and c_y's modifiers. Lastly, we measure *definition overlaps* between c_x and c_y by counting the number of nonstop word overlaps between their definitions obtained by querying *google.com* with "define:c_x" and "define:c_y".

To achieve a comprehensive distance measure for concepts, we propose to effectively combine these features. Our goal is to find a parametric distance metric functions which allows combining various features and assigning different weights for them. It also needs to produce distances that satisfy non-negativity and triangle inequality.

We further estimate W by minimizing the squared errors between the semantic distances d generated from the training data and the expected value $\hat{d}$. Moreover, we constrain W to be PSD. The parameter estimation is:

$$\min_W \sum_{x=1}^{|\mathbf{C}|} \sum_{y=1}^{|\mathbf{C}|} \left(d_{c_x,c_y} - \sqrt{\Phi(c_x,c_y)^T W^{-1} \Phi(c_x,c_y)} \right)^2 \quad (2)$$

subject to $W \succeq 0$. The optimization can be done by any standard semi-definite programming (SDP) solver. We used (Sedumi, 2011) and (Yalmip, 2011) to perform the optimization.

In our framework, the major source of training data is user feedback. Another source is existing hierarchies such as WordNet (Fellbaum, 1998) and ODP (ODP, 2011) (Section 3). Nonetheless, we obtain the semantic distance for a concept pair (c_x, c_y) in training data by summing up edge weights along the shortest path from c_x to c_y in a training hierarchy. The edge weight can be assigned based on the types of relations that an edge represent as in Section 4.1.

The learned model W can be used to predict distance scores for testing concept pairs by applying Eq. 1 on them.

[1]Done by Minipar: http://www.cs.ualberta.ca/lindek/minipar.htm.

[2]Done by Assert: http://cemantix.org/assert/.

3.2 Resolving Path Inconsistency

With the pair-wise semantic distances, we are ready to build the full taxonomy. As in ME, we also take an incremental taxonomy construction framework, where concepts are inserted one at a time. Particularly, we propose that at each insertion, a concept c_z is tried as either a parent or a child concept to all existing nodes in the current partial taxonomy T^n. The evaluation of the best position depends on the semantic distances between c_z and all other concepts in the taxonomy.

To enforce consistency along a path from the root to a leaf in a taxonomy, we propose to require all concepts on the path to be about the same topic. They need to be coherent no matter how far away two concepts are apart in this path. We achieve this by enforcing the sum of semantic distances in a path to be as small as possible. Particularly, when a new concept c_z is added into a taxonomy T, we require that the optimal root-to-leaf path $\hat{P}$ containing c_x should satisfy the following condition:

$$\hat{P_{c_z}} = \arg\min_{P'_{c_z}} \sum_{c_x,c_y \in P'_{c_z}, x<y} d(c_x, c_y) \quad (3)$$

where P_{c_z} is a root-to-leaf path including c_z, $x < y$ defines the order of the concepts so we only compute a pair-wise distance between two concepts once.

To incorporate path consistency into taxonomy construction, we introduce a variable $\lambda \in [0, 1]$ to control the contributions from overall semantic distance minimization (as in ME) and path distance minimization. We formulate the optimization as:

$$\min \lambda u + (1 - \lambda) v \quad (4)$$

subject to $u = |\sum_{c_x,c_y \in C^n \cup \{c_z\}, x<y} d(c_x, c_y) - \sum_{c_x,c_y \in C^n, x<y} d(c_x, c_y)|$, $v = \sum_{c_j,c_k \in P'_{c_z}, j<k} d(c_j, c_k)$, $0 \leq \lambda \leq 1$, where u denotes "minimization of overall semantic distance", v denotes the "path consistency", and C^n is the concept set for the nth partial taxonomy.

4 Resolving Task Specification

Give an arbitrary document collection and its concept set C, most concepts can be organized nicely according to the automatic algorithm proposed in Section 3. However, for concepts with multiple perspectives, we need to decide which perspective the task wants to keep in the browsing taxonomy. Moreover, Section 3 learns distance functions from WordNet and ODP, which suggests that the algorithm will roughly follow how WordNet and ODP define relations. In practice, a task may require completely different organizations, e.g., by question-answer pairs or by topics. The ever-changing task specifications can only be captured by the user/constructor who adjusts a browsing taxonomy to suit the requirements.

This section studies how to incorporate task specifications in the taxonomy construction. Particularly, how to allow the machine learning algorithm to learn from the user, and how to produce a task-specific browsing taxonomy according to the user's guidance. The framework is expected to produce taxonomies that reflect personal preferences as a consequence of learning from manual guidance.

We present a general framework that enables taxonomy construction taking into account user-defined concept organization. Basically, to guide how to organize the concepts, a user trains the supervised distance learning model using a taxonomy construction tool that supports editing functions such as dragging and dropping, adding, deleting, and renaming nodes that allows the user to intuitively modify a taxonomy.

Particularly, an initial taxonomy is constructed by the automatic taxonomy construction framework presented in Section 3. Starting from the initial taxonomy, a user can teach the machine learning algorithm by providing manual guidance to it. The algorithm learns from the manual guidance and adjusts the distance learning function and modifies the taxonomy accordingly. When a user put c_x under c_y, it indicates that the user wants a relation demonstrated by $c_x \rightarrow c_y$ to be true in this taxonomy. We capture the user inputs as *manual guidance* and make use of it to adjust the distance learning model to organize other concepts agreeing with the user. The teaching and the learning alternate until the user is satisfied with the taxonomy. The resulting taxonomy contains both the user's inputs and the machine's adjusted organization for the concepts.

4.1 Collecting and Learning from Manual Guidance

The most challenging part of incorporating manual guidance in the machine learning process is how to translate it into a format that the machine can easily understand and incorporate into its learning models. In this research, browsing taxonomies are tree structures. Trees. however, are not straightforward for a machine learning algorithm to manipulate. In order to capture the changes between each version of the manual editions, the learning algorithm needs both the training and the test data to be in a format which is easy to handle. Matrix representation can be easily understood and manipulated by many machine learning algorithms. We therefore convert taxonomies from trees to matrices and use a matrix representation for all the intermediate editions in the taxonomy construction process.

We propose to convert a taxonomy from a tree to matrices of neighboring nodes and represent the differences in matrices before and after human edits as *manual guidance*. We then train the learning framework to adjust to it and make predictions for unorganized concepts.

We represent the organization of concepts before a user's modifications as a *before matrix*; likewise, the new organization of concepts after her modifications is represented as a *after matrix*. Given these two matrixes, *manual guidance* is a submatrix in *after matrix* that shows the differences between *before matrix* and *after matrix*.

We compare the before matrix *A* and the after matrix *B* to derive the manual guidance *M*. The manual guidance is not simply the matrix difference between the before matrix and the after hierarchy matrix. It is part of the after matrix because it is the after matrix that indicates where the user wants the taxonomy to develop. We define manual guidance M as a submatrix which consists of some entries of the *after matrix* B; at these entries, there exist differences between the *before matrix* A and the *after matrix* B.

For simple cases when the set of concepts remain unchanged before and after human modifications, the above definition and calculation of manual guidance work. However, oftentimes the user adds, deletes or renames concepts, and the concept set changes. When the concept set changes, the above definition of manual guidance M needs a slight alteration.

Figure 1 shows an example taxonomy whose concept set changes. The original concept set before

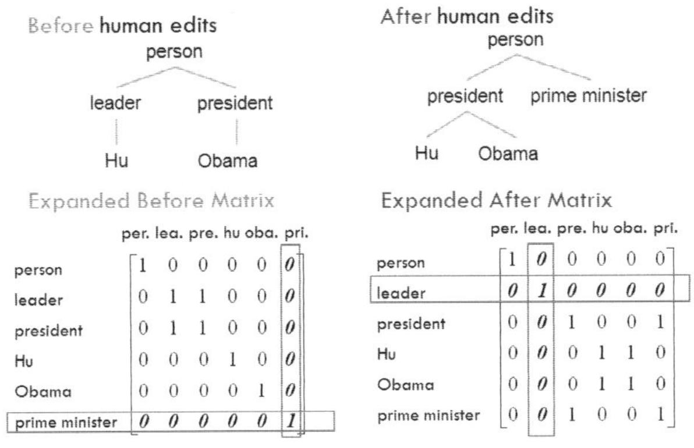

Figure 1: A taxonomy before and after human modifications (concept set changes; relation type = $sibling$).

the human modification is {*person, leader, president, Hu, Obama*}. The taxonomy's *before matrix* A is:

$$A = \begin{array}{c|ccccc} & person & leader & president & Hu & Obama \\ person & 1 & 0 & 0 & 0 & 0 \\ leader & 0 & 1 & 1 & 0 & 0 \\ president & 0 & 1 & 1 & 0 & 0 \\ Hu & 0 & 0 & 0 & 1 & 0 \\ Obama & 0 & 0 & 0 & 0 & 1 \end{array}$$

The user modifies the taxonomy at several places. In particular, *leader* is deleted, *Hu* is moved to be under *president*, and *prime minister* is inserted as a new concept into this taxonomy. Therefore the concept set changes to {*person, president, Hu, Obama, prime minister*}. The *after matrix* B is:

$$B = \begin{array}{c|ccccc} & person & president & Hu & Obama & PM \\ person & 1 & 0 & 0 & 0 & 0 \\ president & 0 & 1 & 0 & 0 & 1 \\ Hu & 0 & 0 & 1 & 1 & 0 \\ Obama & 0 & 0 & 1 & 1 & 0 \\ PM & 0 & 1 & 0 & 0 & 1 \end{array}$$

Since the concept sets before and after the human modifications change, we cannot simply use matrix subtraction to get the difference between the before and after matrices. Suppose the concept set in the taxonomy before the modifications is C_A, and the concept set after modifications is C_B, we define an expanded set of concepts C_E as the union of C_A and C_B.

For taxonomies with concept changes, we define the manual We then define manual guidance M as a submatrix which consists of some entries of the *after matrix* B; at these entries, there exist differences from the *expanded before matrix* A' to the *expanded after matrix* B'. The expanded rows and columns in A' and B' are filled with 0 for non-diagonal entries, and 1 for diagonal entries. Note that the concepts corresponding to these entries should exist in C_B, the unexpanded set of concepts after human modifications. Formally,

$$M = B[r; c]$$

where $r = \{i : b_{ij} - a_{ij} \neq 0, c_i \in C_B\}$, $c = \{j : b_{ij} - a_{ij} \neq 0, c_j \in C_B\}$, a_{ij} is the $(i,j)^{th}$ entry in A', and b_{ij} is the $(i,j)^{th}$ entry in B'.

For the example in Figure 1, the manual guidance M is:

$$M = B[2,3,4,5;2,3,4,5] = \begin{pmatrix} 1 & 0 & 0 & 1 \\ 0 & 1 & 1 & 0 \\ 0 & 1 & 1 & 0 \\ 1 & 0 & 0 & 1 \end{pmatrix}.$$

Based on M, we can create training data $D = 1 - M$, for the supervised distance learning algorithm, which aims to learn a good model which best preserves the regularity defined by the task and the user using the techniques proposed in Section 3.1.

5 Evaluation

To evaluate the effectiveness of our approach, We conducted two user studies, one to evaluate browsing effectiveness and another to evaluate quality of taxonomies. Five users (graduate students and relatives of the authors) in the first study were asked to construct browsing taxonomies with a task in mind - "writing a survey paper about the collection".

In the second study (24 graduates and undergraduates), we compared taxonomies constructed by different users to identify where mixed perspectives in taxonomies come from in Section 5.3. We also investigated whether the differences are due to self-inconsistency in Section 5.4. Moreover, we manually select relations violating path consistency and report our approach's ability to handle path consistency in Section 5.2.

5.1 Datasets

To show that task-specific taxonomies are more suitable for browsing than general taxonomies, we compared excerpts of the official North America Industry Classification Systems (we call them NAICS-

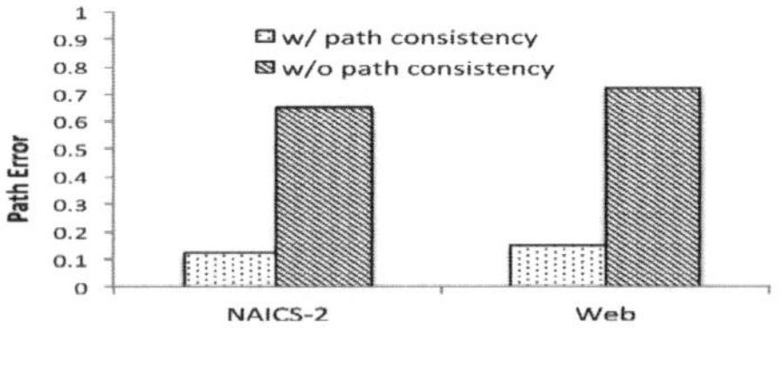

Figure 2: Path error w/ and w/o path consistency control.

1) with comparable taxonomies derived by techniques presented in this paper (we call them NAICS-2). Since the original collection used to build official NAICS taxonomies is not available, we created document collections by crawling search results from *google.com* for concepts in NAICS-1 excerpts. The participants worked on the collection to create NAICS-2 taxonomies. Each NAICS-1 or NAICS-2 taxonomy contains about 40 concepts.

We also evaluate our techniques on Web search result organization. Five Web datasets were created by submitting 4 to 5 queries[3] to and collecting the returned Web documents from search engines Bing and Google. Around 100 Web documents and 40 concepts are collected for a topic. We manually judged relevant documents for each topic.

5.2 Path Consistency

To evaluate how well our method can handle path inconsistency, we compare the path error rate before and after applying path consistency control. The evaluation is only conducted for the automated algorithm (Section 3) on the NAICS-2 and Web datasets. No user study is involved.

Two human assessors manually evaluated the path errors[4] in a taxonomy by the following procedure: (1) Starting from the root concept, perform a depth-first traverse in the taxonomy; (2) along each path, count the number of wrong ancestor-descendant pairs due to word sense ambiguity or mixed perspectives; (3) sum up the errors that both assessors agree and normalize them by the taxonomy size. Note that path errors are evaluated for concepts are *not* immediately connected, whereas differences due to mixed perspectives (Section 5.3) refer to immediate relations. Figure 2 shows that with path consistency control, we can statistically significantly reduce path errors due to word sense ambiguity and mixed perspectives by 500% (p-value$<$.001, t-test). It strongly indicates that our technique to control path inconsistency in taxonomy construction is effective.

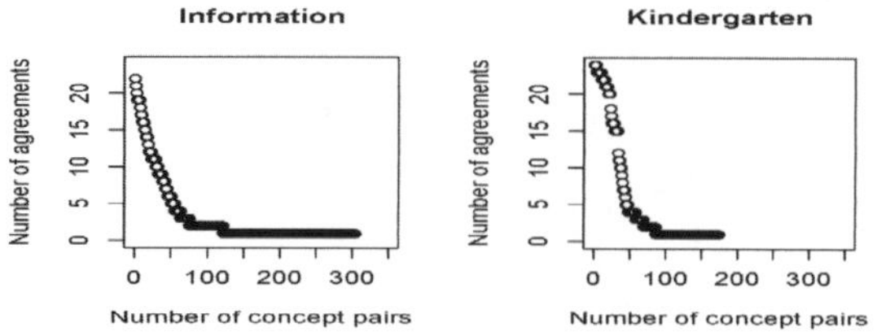

Figure 3: Agreements among participants for the parent-child pairs for datasets *information* and *kindergarten*.

5.3 Mixed Perspectives in Taxonomies

To better understand mixed perspectives in taxonomies constructed, we look for commonality and differences among the taxonomies constructed by the 24 participants for the same topic in the second user study. We break each taxonomy into parent-child pairs, and count how many participants agreed on a pair. The agreements range from 1 to 24. The taxonomies we examined are NAICS-2 and Web.

We plot the number of agreements for every concept pair and observe a long-tail power-law distribution for all datasets. Figure 3 shows that for the dataset "information", which contains about 300 unique concept pairs, while in "kindergarten", more than 200 unique concept pairs exist. This suggests that people use rich and diverse expressions to construct taxonomies and organize information differently within them. Although commonality (can be as high as 24 out of 24) and differences co-exist in taxonomies created for the same topic, the differences are much more dominate than the commonality.

We manually break down the types of differences in producing parent-child pairs into the following categories: *mixed parents* (a concept has different parent concepts due to word sense ambiguity), *mixed ancestors* (a concept is assigned to grandparents, not the direct parent), *mixed relation types* (a pair show relations other than *is-a*, such as part-of and affiliation), *new concepts* (participants add new concepts), *morphological differences* (plurals, -tion, etc), *errors* (clearly wrong relations, e.g.,

[3]E.g., queries "trip to DC", "Washington DC", "DC", and "Washington" were submitted for the topic "plan a trip to DC".

[4]Other types of errors were ignored in the assessment.

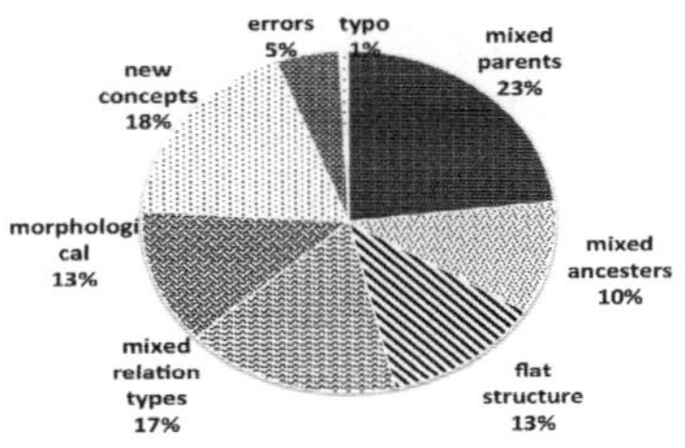

Figure 4: Sources of differences in NAICS-2 and Web.

infant→school director), *flat structure* (some participants liked to assign a large portion of concepts as children to the root), and *typo*.

Figure 4 illustrates the break-down of various types of differences. *Mixed parents* is the largest contributor with 23% share, followed by *new concepts* (18%) and *mixed relation types* (17%). Among all the types, *mixed parents*, *new concepts*, and *mixed relation types* indicate mixed perspectives or word sense ambiguity; in total they contribute about 58% differences in taxonomies. *Flat structure* and *mixed ancestors* are about confusions in taxonomy topology, which contribute about 23% differences. Other differences due to morphological changes, typos and errors contribute about 19% differences. The break-down reveals that mixed perspective, one of main foci in this paper, is indeed the biggest source of difference in taxonomy construction.

5.4 Self-agreement

Another doubt is that maybe the differences come from randomness? To find out if the variations among taxonomies is due to randomness, we designed a repeat phase in the second user study. We randomly invited 12 participants to repeat the same tasks in the same order 3 weeks[5] after the initial phase and compare the taxonomies constructed in both phases for the NAICS-2 and Web datasets.

We use Fragment-Based Similarity (FBS) proposed by (Yang, 2011) to calculate the similarity between taxonomies constructed in the initial phase and in the repeat phase by the same participant. FBS for two taxonomies T_i and T_j is calculated as: $FBS(T_i, T_j) = \frac{1}{max(U,V)} \sum_{p=1}^{m} sim_{cos}(t_{ip}, t_{jp})$, where U and V is the number of concepts in T_i and T_j respectively, m is the number of matched pairs based on the highest cosine similarity, sim_{cos} is the cosine similarity between vectors for subtrees of concepts t_ip and t_jp.

[5]The three week period ensured that participants only had limited memory of the details about the tasks.

Self agreement (in FBS)	Max	Min	Average
per participant per dataset	1	0.37	0.74
per participant	0.81	0.63	0.74
per dataset	0.95	0.62	0.74

Table 1: Self-agreement; measured in FBS.

Table 1 indicate the self-agreement between taxonomies for any participant and/or any topic. The max self-agreement is as high as 1. The average self-agreement is 0.74, which is high at the range of FBS. It suggests that the participants are quite self-consistent when constructing taxonomies at different times. It builds the foundation for our study on multiple perspectives in taxonomy construction.

6 Conclusion

This paper explores techniques to *quickly* derive *task-specific* taxonomies supporting browsing in arbitrary document sets. It addresses two issues in taxonomy construction: path inconsistency due to word sense ambiguity and mixed perspectives, and task specifications in arbitrary collections. We tackle both issues in a supervised distance learning framework via minimizing distances along a path and using user inputs as training data, respectively. The user studies strongly suggest that the proposed techniques are highly effective in constructing browsing taxonomies as well as handling path consistency.

References

J. R. Bellegarda, J. W. Butzberger, Yen-Lu Chow, N. B. Coccaro, and D. Naik. 1996. A novel word clustering algorithm based on latent semantic analysis. In *Proceedings of the Acoustics, Speech, and Signal Processing, 1996. on Conference Proceedings., 1996 IEEE International Conference - Volume 01*, ICASSP '96, pages 172–175, Washington, DC, USA. IEEE Computer Society.

Matthew Berland and Eugene Charniak. 1999. Finding parts in very large corpora. In *Proceedings of the 27th Annual Meeting for the Association for Computational Linguistics (ACL 1999)*.

Rajendra Bhatia. 2006. *Positive definite matrices (princeton series in applied mathematics)*. Princeton University Press, December.

Claudio Carpineto, Stefano Mizzaro, Giovanni Romano, and Matteo Snidero. 2009. Mobile information retrieval with search results clustering: Prototypes and evaluations. *Journal of American Society for Information Science and Technology (JASIST)*, pages 877–895.

Duen Horng Chau, Aniket Kittur, Jason I. Hong, and Christos Faloutsos. 2011. Apolo: making sense of large network data by combining rich user interaction and machine learning. In *CHI*, pages 167–176.

Gouglass R. Cutting, David R. Karger, Jan R. Petersen, and John W. Tukey. 1992. Scatter/Gather: A cluster-based approach to browsing large document collections. In *Proceedings of the fifteenth Annual ACM Conference on Research and Development in Information Retrieval (SIGIR 1992)*.

Oren Etzioni, Michael Cafarella, Doug Downey, Ana-Maria Popescu, Tal Shaked, Stephen Soderland, Daniel S. Weld, and Alexander Yates. 2005. Unsupervised named-entity extraction from the web: an experimental study. In *Artificial Intelligence, 165(1):91-134, June*.

Christiane Fellbaum. 1998. *WordNet: an electronic lexical database*. MIT Press.

Roxana Girju, Adriana Badulescu, and Dan Moldovan. 2003. Learning semantic constraints for the automatic discovery of part-whole relations. In *Proceedings of the Human Language Technology Conference/Annual Conference of the North American Chapter of the Association for Computational Linguistics (HLT/NAACL 2003)*.

Marti A. Hearst. 1992. Automatic acquisition of hyponyms from large text corpora. In *Proceedings of the 14th International Conference on Computational Linguistics (COLING 1992)*.

Zornitsa Kozareva and Eduard Hovy. 2010. A semi-supervised method to learn and construct taxonomies using the web. In *Proceedings of the 2010 Conference on Empirical Methods in Natural Language Processing*, pages 1110–1118, Cambridge, MA, October. Association for Computational Linguistics.

Zornitsa Kozareva, Ellen Riloff, and Eduard Hovy. 2008. Semantic class learning from the web with hyponym pattern linkage graphs. In *Proceedings of the 46th Annual Meeting for the Association for Computational Linguistics (ACL 2008)*.

Krishna Kummamuru, Rohit Lotlikar, Shourya Roy, Karan Singal, and Raghu Krishnapuram. 2004. A hierarchical monothetic document clustering algorithm for summarization and browsing search results. *Proceedings of the 13th conference on World Wide Web WWW 04*, page 658.

Dawn Lawrie, W. Bruce Croft, and Arnold Rosenberg. 2001. Finding topic words for hierarchical summarization. In *Proceedings of the 24th Annual ACM Conference on Research and Development in Information Retrieval (SIGIR 2001)*, pages 349–357.

LCSH. 2011. Library of congress subject headings. `http://www.loc.gov/`.

P. C. Mahalanobis. 1936. On the generalised distance in statistics. In *Proceedings of the National Institute of Sciences of India 2 (1): 495*.

ODP. 2011. Open directory project. `http://www.dmoz.org/`.

Patrick Pantel and Marco Pennacchiotti. 2006. Espresso: Leveraging generic patterns for automatically harvesting semantic relations. In *Proceedings of the 44th Annual Meeting for the Association for Computational Linguistics (ACL 2006)*.

Deepak Ravichandran and Eduard Hovy. 2002. Learning surface text patterns for a question answering system. In *Proceedings of the 40th Annual Meeting for the Association for Computational Linguistics (ACL 2002)*.

Mark Sanderson and W. Bruce Croft. 1999. Deriving concept hierarchies from text. In *Proceedings of the 22nd Annual International ACM SIGIR Conference on Research and Development in Information Retrieval (SIGIR 1999)*.

Sedumi. 2011. `http://sedumi.mcmaster.ca`.

Rion Snow, Daniel Jurafsky, and Andrew Y. Ng. 2006. Semantic taxonomy induction from heterogenous evidence. In *Proceedings of the 21st International Conference on Computational Linguistics and 44th Annual Meeting of the Association for Computational Linguistics (ACL/COLING 2006)*.

Yalmip. 2011. `http://users.isy.liu.se/johanl/yalmip`.

Hui Yang and Jamie Callan. 2009. A metric-based framework for automatic taxonomy induction. In *Proceedings of the 47th Annual Meeting for the Association for Computational Linguistics (ACL 2009)*.

Hui Yang. 2011. *Personalized Concept Hierarchy Construction*. Ph.D. thesis, Carnegie Mellon University. `http://www.cs.cmu.edu/~huiyang/publication/dissertation.pdf`.

EAGER: Extending Automatically Gazetteers for Entity Recognition

Omer Gunes, Christian Schallhart, Tim Furche
Department of Computer Science,
Oxford University, Oxford OX1 3QD
firstname.lastname@cs.ox.ac.uk

Jens Lehmann, Axel Ngonga
Institute of Computer Science,
University of Leipzig, 04103 Leipzig
lastname@informatik.uni-leipzig.de

Abstract

Key to named entity recognition, the manual gazetteering of entity lists is a costly, error-prone process that often yields results that are incomplete and suffer from sampling bias. Exploiting current sources of structured information, we propose a novel method for extending minimal seed lists into complete gazetteers. Like previous approaches, we value WIKIPEDIA as a huge, well-curated, and relatively unbiased source of entities. However, in contrast to previous work, we exploit not only its content, but also its structure, as exposed in DBPEDIA. We extend gazetteers through Wikipedia categories, carefully limiting the impact of noisy categorizations. The resulting gazetteers easily outperform previous approaches on named entity recognition.

1 Introduction

Automatically learning gazetteers with minimal supervision is a long standing problem in named entity recognition.

We propose EAGER as a novel approach to extending automatically gazetteers for entity recognition, utilizing DBPEDIA (Bizer et al., 2009) rather than WIKIPEDIA. DBPEDIA serves as a much better foundation than WIKIPEDIA, because all the information used in previous approaches (and much more) is already provided as a structured database of facts and articles. The extraction is more robust and complete than ad-hoc methods and maintained by a large community. E.g., navigating the category hierarchy is much easier and reliable with DBPEDIA.

To summarize, EAGER's main contributions are

(1) A *novel gazetteer expansion algorithm* that adds new entities from DBPEDIA. EAGER adds entities that have several categories in common with the seed terms, addressing noisy categorizations through a sophisticated *category pruning technique.*

(2) EAGER also extracts categories from DBPEDIA abstracts using *dependency analysis.* Finally, EAGER extracts plural forms and synonyms from *redirect information.*

(3) For *entity recognition*, we integrate the gazetteer with a simple, but effective machine learning classifier, and *experimentally* show that the extended gazetteers improve the F_1 score between 7% and 12% over our baseline approach and outperform (Zhang and Iria, 2009) on all learned concepts (subject, location, temporal).

2 Related Work

We divide the related work in automatic gazetteer population into three groups: **(1)** *Machine learning* approaches **(2)** *Pattern driven* approaches Finally, like our own work, **(3)** *knowledge driven* approaches

Knowledge Driven. In any case, machine learning and pattern driven approaches extract their terms from unstructured sources – despite the fact that large, general knowledge bases became available in the last years. One of the first knowledge-driven methods (Magnini et al., 2002) employed WORDNET to identify trigger words and candidate gazetteer terms with its word-class and -instance relations. As WORDNET covers domain specific vocabularies only to a limited extent, this approach is also limited in its general applicability.

In (Toral and Muñoz, 2006), gazetteers are built from the noun phrases in the first sentences of WIKIPEDIA articles by mapping these phrases to WORDNET and adding further terms found along the hypernymy relations. The approach presented in (Kazama and Torisawa, 2007; Kazama and Torisawa, 2008) relies solely on WIKIPEDIA, producing gazetteers without explicitly named concepts, arguing that consistent but anonymous labels are still useful.

Most closely related to our own work, the authors of (Zhang and Iria, 2009) build an approach solely on WIKIPEDIA which does not only exploit the article text but also analyzes the structural elements of WIKIPEDIA:

Algorithm 1: `GazetteerExtension`($\mathscr{S}$)

1 **foreach** *seed entity* $e \in \mathscr{S}$ **do**
2   find article a for e in DBPEDIA;
3     $\mathsf{Articles}(e) \leftarrow a$;
4 $\mathscr{G} \leftarrow \emptyset$; $\mathscr{P} \leftarrow \emptyset$;
5 **foreach** *entity e, article* $a = \mathsf{Articles}(e)$ **do**
6   **foreach** *sentence* $s \in a.\mathsf{Abstract}$ **do**
7         $D_s \leftarrow$ dependencies in s;
8   add all t : $\mathsf{nsubj}(e,t) \in D_s$ to $\mathscr{P}$;
9   add all t : $\mathsf{nsubj}(e,t'), \mathsf{conj}(t',t) \in D_s$ to $\mathscr{P}$;
10   **foreach** *article* $a' \in a.\mathsf{Redirects}$ **do**
11   add all labels of a to $\mathscr{G}$;
12     $\mathsf{Cats}(e) \leftarrow \mathsf{Cats}(e) \cup a.\mathsf{Cats}$;
13 **foreach** *entity e, category* $c \in \mathsf{Cats}(e)$ **do**
14     $\mathsf{Cats}(e) \leftarrow \mathsf{Cats}(e) \cup \mathtt{CategoryNeighbors}(c,k)$;
15 **foreach** *category* $c \in \mathsf{Cats}(e)$ *for some e* **do**
16     $\mathsf{Support}(c) \leftarrow |\{e' : c \in \mathsf{Cats}(e')\}|$;
17 **foreach** *connected component* $\mathscr{C}$ *in* Cats **do**
18     $\mathsf{Support}(\mathscr{C}) \leftarrow \sum_{c \in \mathscr{C}} \mathsf{Support}(c)$;
19 MaxCatComp $\leftarrow \mathscr{C}$ with maximal Support;
20 add all categories in MaxCatComp to $\mathscr{P}$;
21 **foreach** *category* $c \in \mathscr{P}$ **do**
22   **foreach** *article a with* $c \in a.\mathsf{Cats}$ **do**
23   **if** $|a.\mathsf{Cats} \setminus \mathscr{P}| \leq \theta$ **then**
24   add all labels of a to $\mathscr{G}$;

3 Automatically Extending Gazetteer Lists

3.1 Extraction Algorithm: Overview

Algorithm 1 shows an outline of the gazetteer expansion algorithm used in EAGER. To extend an initial seed set $\mathscr{S}$ EAGER proceeds, roughly, in three steps: First, it identifies DBPEDIA articles for seed entities and extracts implicit category and synonym information from abstracts and redirect information (Lines 1–11). Second, it finds additional categories from the DBPEDIA category hierarchy (Lines 12–20). Finally, it uses the categories from the first two steps to extract additional entities (Lines 21–24). In the following, we consider the three steps separately.

3.2 Implicit: Abstract and Redirects

Before EAGER can analyse abstract and redirect information for an article, we need to **find the corresponding DBPEDIA articles** (Lines 1–3) for each seed entry in $\mathscr{S}$. There may be one or more such entry. Here, we observe the first advantage of DBPEDIA's more structured information: DBPEDIA already contains plain text labels such as "Barack Obama" and we can directly query (using the SPARQL endpoint) all articles with a label equal (or starting with) an entity in our seed set. This allows for more precise article matching and avoids complex URL encodings as necessary in previous, WIKIPEDIA-based approaches such as (Kazama and Torisawa, 2007). As (Zhang and Iria, 2009), we reject redirection entries in this step as ambiguous.

With the articles identified, we can proceed to extract category information from the abstracts and new entities from the redirect information. In the **dependency analysis of article abstracts** (Lines 6–9), we aim to extract category (or, more generally, hypernym) information from the abstracts of articles on the ssed list. We perform a standard dependency analysis on the sentences of the abstract and return all nouns that stand in `nsubj` relation to a seed entity or (directly or indirectly) in `conj` (correlative conjunction) relation to a noun that stands in `nsubj` relation to a seed entity. This allows us to extract, e.g., both "general" and "statesman" as categories from a sentence such as "Julius Caesar was a Roman general and statesman". This analysis is inspired by (Zhang and Iria, 2009), but performed on the entire abstract which is clearly dis-

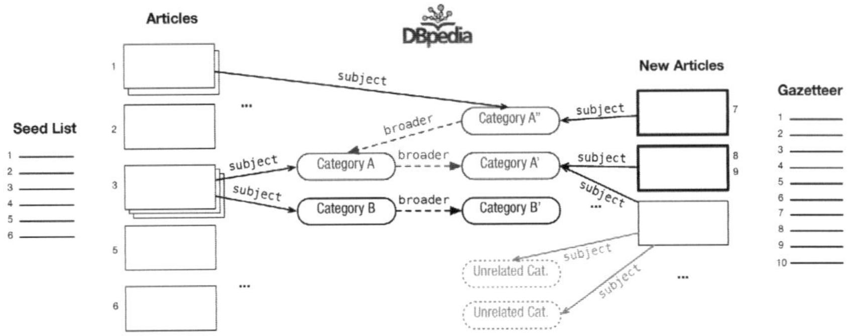

Figure 1: EAGER Gazetteer Extension Algorithm

tinguished in WIKIPEDIA. This contrasts to (Zhang and Iria, 2009), where this is applied only to the first sentence (as WIKIPEDIA does not directly provide a concept of "abstract"). All categories thus obtained are added to $\mathscr{P}$ and will be used in Section 3.4 to generate additional entities.

Finally, we are interested in **redirection information** (Lines 10–11) about an article for a seed entity as that provides such with synonyms, plural forms, different spellings, etc. Fortunately, DBPEDIA provides this information directly by means of the `dbpedia-owl:wikiPageRedirects` property. The labels of all redirect articles with this property pointing to a seed entity articles are directly added to the Gazetteer.

3.3 Explicit: Category Graph

In addition to categories from the abstract analysis, we also use the **category graph** of DBPEDIA. It has been previously observed, (Zhang and Iria, 2009) and (Strube and Ponzetto, 2006), that the category graph of poor quality. DBPEDIA improves little on that fact. However, EAGER uses a sophisticated analysis of categories related to seed entities that allows us to prune most of the noise in the category graph. Biased towards precision over recall, Section 4 shows that combined with the category extraction from abstracts it provides a significantly extended Gazetteer without introducing substantial noise.

The fundamental contribution of EAGER is a category pruning based on finding a connected component in the graph of related categories that is supported by as many different entities from the seed list as possible. Figure 1 illustrates this further: From the articles for the seed entities, we compute (Line 12) the direct categories (via `subject` edges) and associate them to their seed entities e via $\texttt{Cats}(e)$. We extent this set (Lines 13–14) with all categories in the k-neighbourhood (here, we use $k = 3$), i.e., connected via up to k `broader` edges traversed in any direction, again maintaining via $\texttt{Cats}(e)$ which categories are reached from which seed entity e. In the resulting graph of all such categories, we identify the connected component with *maximum support* (Lines 15–19). The support of a component is the sum of the support of its categories. The support of a category c is the number of seed entities with $c \in \texttt{Cats}(e)$. For Figure 1, this yields the category graph of the blue and black categories of the figure. The blue categories form the connected component with maximum support and are thus retained (in $\mathscr{P}$), the black categories are dropped.

3.4 Entities from Categories

Finally, in Lines 21–24, EAGER completes the gazetteer extension by extracting the labels of all articles of categories in $\mathscr{P}$ if they are *sufficiently unambiguous*. An article is called sufficiently unambiguous, if it is categorised only with categories from $\mathscr{P}$ up to a threshold θ (here, set to 5) of non-$\mathscr{P}$ categories. This avoids adding very general entities that tend to have large number of categories in WIKIPEDIA and thus DBPEDIA. The output of Algorithm 3 is the extended gazetteers $\mathscr{G}$.

4 Evaluation

To evaluate the impact of EAGER on entity recognition, we performed a large set of experiments (on the archeology domain). The experiment domains and

	Subject			Location			Temporal		
	P	*R*	F_1	*P*	*R*	F_1	*P*	*R*	F_1
Baseline (B)	69.9	54.1	62.0	76.5	46.1	61.3	86.4	75.4	80.9
B+ Dependency	73.6	64.7	69.0	73.4	69.4	71.4	86.2	85.2	85.7
B+ Category	72.3	64.5	68.5	71.9	70.1	71.0	86.4	85.0	85.8
B+ Redirection	71.6	65.8	68.7	71.2	71.7	71.4	86.32	85.46	85.89
(Zhang and Iria, 2009) full	69.8	66.5	68.1	68.9	75.0	71.8	82.4	83.4	82.9
EAGER *full*	72.1	66.5	69.3	72.0	74.6	73.3	86.8	86.1	86.5

Table 1: EAGER comparison

corpora are described in Section 4.1. Finally, Section 4.2 presents the results of the evaluation, showing the contributions of the different parts of EAGER and comparing it with (Zhang and Iria, 2009), which we outperform for all entity types, in some cases up to 5% in F_1 score.

4.1 Evaluation Setup

In this experiment, we consider entity recognition in the domain of archaeology.

As part of this effort, (Jeffrey et al., 2009) identified three types of entities that are most useful for archaeological research; Subject(SUB), Temporal Terms(TEM), Location (LOC).

In this evaluation, we use the same setup as in (Zhang and Iria, 2009): A corpus of 30 full length UK archaeological reports archived by the Arts and Humanities Data Service (AHDS). The length of the documents varies from 4 to 120 pages. The corpus is inter-annotated by three archaeologists.

4.2 Result

For the evaluation, we perform a 5-fold validation on the above corpus. The evaluate the performance (in terms of precision, recall and F_1 score) for entity recognition of the baseline system as well as the baseline system extended with a gazetteer feature. For the latter, we consider full EAGER as described in Section 3 as well as only the entities derived from dependency analysis of abstracts, from the category graph, and from redirection information. Finally, we also include the performance numbers report in (Zhang and Iria, 2009) for comparison (since we share their evaluation settings).

Table 1 show the results of the comparison: EAGER significantly improves precision and recall over the baseline system and outperforms(Zhang and Iria, 2009) in all cases. Furthermore, the impact of all three types of information (dependencies from abstract, category, redirection) of EAGER individually is quite notable with a slight disadvantage for category information. However, in all cases the combination of all three types as proposed in EAGER shows a significant further increase in performance.

5 Conclusion

At its heart, EAGER is a novel algorithm for extending sets of entities of a specific type with additional entities of that type extracted from DBPEDIA. It is based on a new strategy for pruning the category graph in DBPEDIA (and thus WIKIPEDIA), necessary to address the inherent noise. Our evaluation shows that EAGER can significantly improve the performance of entity recognition and outperforms existing systems in all cases. Unlike previous approaches, our approach makes use of richer content and structural elements of DBpedia.

We believe that EAGER is a strong indicator that DBPEDIA provides a much richer, yet easier to use foundation for NLP tasks in general than WIKIPEDIA.

The extensibility and domain adaptability of our methods still need further investigation. We are currently extending the evaluation to several other domains, including property descriptions in real estate and classified adds. We are also investigating more targeted means of detecting and addressing noise in the category graph.

References

Christian Bizer, Jens Lehmann, Georgi Kobilarov, Sören Auer, Christian Becker, Richard Cyganiak, and Sebastian Hellmann. 2009. DBpedia – A crystallization point for the Web of Data. *Web Semantics: Science, Services and Agents on the World Wide Web*, 7(3).

Stuart Jeffrey, Julian Richards, Fabio Ciravegna, Stewart Waller, Sam Chapman, and Ziqi Zhang. 2009. The Archaeotools project: Faceted Classification and Natural Language Processing in an Archaeological Context. *Phil. Trans. R. Soc. A*, 367(3):2507–2519.

Jun'ichi Kazama and Kentaro Torisawa. 2007. Exploiting Wikipedia as External Knowledge for Named Entity Recognition. In *Proceedings of the 2007 Joint Conference on Empirical Methods in Natural Language Processing and Computational Natural Language Learning*, EMNLP-CoNLL, pages 698–707.

Jun'ichi Kazama and Kentaro Torisawa. 2008. Inducing Gazetteers for Named Entity Recognition by Large-Scale Clustering of Dependency Relations. In *Proceedings of the 46th Annual Meeting of the Association for Computational Linguistics (ACL)*, pages 407–415.

Bernardo Magnini, Matteo Negri, Roberto Prevete, and Hristo Tanev. 2002. A WordNet-based approach to Named Entities recognition. In *Proceedings of the 2002 workshop on Building and using semantic networks - Volume 11*, SEMANET '02, pages 1–7.

M. Strube and S. P. Ponzetto. 2006. WikiRelate! Computing Semantic Relatedness Using Wikipedia. In *Proceedings of the 21st National Conference on Artificial Intelligence*, pages 1419–1424.

Antonio Toral and Rafael Muñoz. 2006. A Proposal to Automatically Build and Maintain Gazetteers for Named Entity Recognition by using Wikipedia. In *Proceedings of the Workshop on New Text – wikis and blogs and other Dynamic text sources*, ECAL'06, pages 56–61.

Ziqi Zhang and José Iria. 2009. A novel approach to automatic gazetteer generation using Wikipedia. In *Proceedings of the 2009 Workshop on The People's Web Meets NLP: Collaboratively Constructed Semantic Resources*, People's Web '09, pages 1–9.

Extracting Context-Rich Entailment Rules from Wikipedia Revision History

Elena Cabrio
INRIA
2004, route de Lucioles BP93
06902 Sophia Antipolis, France.
elena.cabrio@inria.fr

Bernardo Magnini
FBK
Via Sommarive 18
38100 Povo-Trento, Italy.
magnini@fbk.eu

Angelina Ivanova
University of Oslo
Gaustadalléen 23B
Ole-Johan Dahls hus
N-0373 Oslo, Norway.
angelii@ifi.uio.no

Abstract

Recent work on Textual Entailment has shown a crucial role of knowledge to support entailment inferences. However, it has also been demonstrated that currently available entailment rules are still far from being optimal. We propose a methodology for the automatic acquisition of large scale context-rich entailment rules from Wikipedia revisions, taking advantage of the syntactic structure of entailment pairs to define the more appropriate linguistic constraints for the rule to be successfully applicable. We report on rule acquisition experiments on Wikipedia, showing that it enables the creation of an innovative (i.e. acquired rules are not present in other available resources) and good quality rule repository.

1 Introduction

Entailment rules have been introduced to provide pieces of knowledge that may support entailment judgments (Dagan *et al.*, 2009) with some degree of confidence. More specifically, an entailment rule is defined (Szpektor *et al.*, 2007) as a directional relation between two sides of a pattern, corresponding to text fragments with variables (typically phrases or parse sub-trees). The left-hand side (LHS) of the pattern entails the right-hand side (RHS) of the same pattern under the same variable instantiation. Given the Text-Hypothesis pair (T-H) in Example 1:

Example 1.

T: *Dr. Thomas Bond established a hospital in Philadelphia for the reception and cure of poor sick persons.*

H: *Dr. Bond created a medical institution for sick people.*

a (directional) lexical rule like:

1) **LHS:** *hospital* $\Rightarrow$ **RHS:** *medical institution*
probability: 0.8

brings to a TE system (aimed at recognizing that a particular target meaning can be inferred from different text variants in several NLP application, e.g. Question Answering or Information Extraction) the knowledge that the word *hospital* in Text can be aligned, or transformed, into the word *medical institution* in the Hypothesis, with a probability 0.8 that this operation preserves the entailment relation among T and H. Similar considerations apply for more complex rules involving verbs, as:

2) **LHS:** *X establish Y* $\Rightarrow$ **RHS:** *X create Y*
probability: 0.8

where the variables may be instantiated by any textual element with a specified syntactic relation with the verb. Both kinds of rules are typically acquired either from structured sources (e.g. WordNet (Fellbaum, 1998)), or from unstructured sources according for instance to distributional properties (e.g. DIRT (Lin and Pantel, 2001)). Entailment rules should typically be applied only in specific contexts, defined in (Szpektor *et al.*, 2007) as *relevant contexts*. Some existing paraphrase and entailment acquisition algorithms add constraints to the learned rules (e.g. (Sekine, 2005), (Callison-Burch, 2008)), but most do not. Because of a lack of an adequate representation of the linguistic context in which the rules can be successfully applied, their concrete use reflects this limitation. For instance, rule 2 (extracted from DIRT) fails if applied to "The mathematician established the validity of the conjecture", where the sense of *establish* is not a synonym of *create* (but of *prove, demonstrate*), decreasing system's precision. Moreover, these rules often suffer from lack of directionality, and from low accuracy (i.e. the strength of association of the two sides of the rule is often weak, and not well defined). Such observations are also in line with the discussion on ablation tests carried out at the last RTE evaluation campaigns (Bentivogli *et al.*, 2010).

Additional constraints specifying the variable types are therefore required to correctly instantiate them. In this work, we propose to take advantage of Collaboratively Constructed Semantic Resources (CSRs) (namely, Wikipedia) to mine information useful to context-rich entailment rule acquisition. More specifically, we take advantage of material obtained through Wikipedia revisions, which provides at the same time real textual variations from which we may extrapolate the relevant syntactic context, and several simplifications with respect to alternative resources. We consider T-H pairs where T is a revision of a Wikipedia sentence and H is the original sentence, as the revision is considered more informative then the revised sentence.

We demonstrate the feasibility of the proposed approach for the acquisition of context-rich rules from Wikipedia revision pairs, focusing on two case studies, i.e. the acquisition of entailment rules for *causality* and for *temporal expressions*. Both phenomena are highly frequent in TE pairs, and for both there are no available resources yet. The result of our experiments consists in a repository that can be used by TE systems, and that can be easily extended to entailment rules for other phenomena.

The paper is organized as follows. Section 2 reports on previous work, highlighting the specificity of our work. Section 3 motivates and describes the general principles underlying our acquisition methodology. Section 4 describes in details the steps for context-rich rules acquisition from Wikipedia pairs. Section 5 reports about the experiments on causality and temporal expressions and the obtained results. Finally, Section 6 concludes the paper and suggests directions for future improvements.

2 Related work

The use of Wikipedia revision history in NLP tasks has been previously investigated by a few works. In (Zanzotto and Pennacchiotti, 2010), two versions of Wikipedia and semi-supervised machine learning methods are used to extract large TE data sets similar to the ones provided for the RTE challenges. (Yatskar *et al.*, 2010) focus on using edit histories in Simple English Wikipedia to extract lexical simplifications. Nelken and Yamangil (2008) compare different versions of the same document to collect users' editorial choices, for automated text correction, sentence compression and text summarization systems. (Max and Wisniewski, 2010) use the revision history of French Wikipedia to create a corpus of natural rewritings, including spelling corrections, reformulations, and other local text transformations. In (Dutrey *et al.*, 2011), a subpart of this corpus is analyzed to define a typology of local modifications.

Because of its high coverage, Wikipedia is used by the TE community for lexical-semantic rules acquisition, named entity recognition, geographical information[1] (e.g. (Mehdad *et al.*, 2009), (Mirkin *et al.*, 2009), (Iftene and Moruz, 2010)), i.e. to provide TE systems with world and background knowledge. However, so far it has only been used as source of factual knowledge, while in our work the focus is on the acquisition of more complex rules, concerning for instance spatial or temporal expressions.

The interest of the research community in producing specific methods to collect inference and paraphrase pairs is proven by a number of works in the field, which are relevant to the proposed approach.

As for paraphrase, Sekine's Paraphrase Database (Sekine, 2005) is collected using an unsupervised method, and focuses on phrases connecting two Named Entities. In the Microsoft Research Paraphrase Corpus[2], pairs of sentences are extracted from news sources on the web, and manually annotated. As for rule repositories collected using distributional properties, DIRT (Discovery of Inference Rules from Text)[3] is a collection of inference rules

[1] http://www.aclweb.org/aclwiki/index.php?title=RTE_Knowledge_Resources

[2] http://research.microsoft.com/en-us/downloads

[3] http://www.aclweb.org/aclwiki/index.php?title=DIRT_Paraphrase_Collection

(Lin and Pantel, 2001), obtained extracting binary relations between a verb and an object-noun (or a small clause) from dependency trees. Barzilay and Lee (2003) present an approach for generating sentence level paraphrases, learning structurally similar patterns of expression from data and identifying paraphrasing pairs among them using a comparable corpus. Since the data sets cited so far are paraphrase collections, rules are bidirectional, while one of the peculiarities of the entailment relation is the directionality, addressed in our work.

Aharon *et al.* (2010) presented FRED, an algorithm for generating entailment rules between predicates from FrameNet. Moreover, the TEASE collection of entailment rules (Szpektor *et al.*, 2004) consists of 136 templates provided as input, plus all the learned templates. Their web-based extraction algorithm is applied to acquire verb-based expressions. No directionality of the pairs is specified, but additional guessing mechanisms it are proposed. In (Szpektor and Dagan, 2008), two approaches for unsupervised learning of *unary* rules (i.e. between templates with a single variable) are investigated.

In (Zhao *et al.*, 2009), a pivot approach for extracting paraphrase patterns from bilingual parallel corpora is presented, while in (Callison-Burch, 2008) the quality of paraphrase extraction from parallel corpora is improved by requiring that phrases and their paraphrases have the same syntactic type. Our approach is different from theirs in many respects: their goal is paraphrase extraction, while we are extracting directional entailment rules; as textual resources for pattern extraction they use parallel corpora (using patterns in another language as pivots), while we rely on monolingual Wikipedia revisions (taking benefit from its increasing size); the paraphrases they extract are more similar to DIRT, while our approach allows to focus on the acquisition of rules for specific phenomena frequent in entailment pairs, and not covered by other resources.

3 General methodology

The general approach we have implemented is based on the idea that, given a *seed word*, we extract all the entailment rules from Wikipedia revision pairs where the seed word appears as the head of the rule either in T or H. The head is the non-variable part of the rule on which the other parts depend (i.e. the word *establish* is the head of rule 2).

Entailment judgment. A Wikipedia revision may be consistent with the original sentence, bringing to an entailment relation, or it may introduce inconsistency, expressing a contradiction w.r.t. the original sentence. We manually checked a sample of revision pairs ($\sim$200), and we found out that in about 95% of the revisions entailment is preserved, in line with (Zanzotto and Pennacchiotti, 2010). We assume this one as the default case in our experiments.

Monothematic pairs. The capability of automatic extraction of entailment rules is affected by the complexity of the pairs from which we extract the rules. In our experiments we take advantage of revision pairs with minimal difference between T and H, and we assume that for such pairs we have only one rule to extract. Under this perspective, T-H pairs derived from Wikipedia revisions have strong similarity with *monothematic pairs* (i.e. pairs where the entailment judgment is due to only one linguistic phenomenon, as suggested in (Bentivogli *et al.*, 2010)). Section 4.2 describes the algorithm for filtering out revision pairs with more than one phenomenon.

Directionality. A Wikipedia revision, in principle, may be interpreted as either T entailing H, or as H entailing T. However, through a manual inspection of a revision sample ($\sim$200 pairs), it came out that in most of the cases the meaning of the revised sentence (T) entails the meaning of the original one (H). Given such observation, for our experiments (Sections 4 and 5) we assume that for all revision pairs, the revised sentence (T) entails the original one (H).

Context of a rule. We have defined the notion of context of a rule R as a set of morpho-syntactic constraints C over the application of R in a specific T-H pair. Ideally, the set of such constraints should be the minimal set of constraints over R such that the proportion of successful applications of R is maximized (e.g. the precision-recall mean is highest). Intuitively, given an entailment rule, in absence of constraints we have the highest recall (the rule is always applied when the LHS is activated in T and the RHS is activated in H), although we may find cases of wrong application of the rule (i.e. low precision). On the other side, as syntactic constraints are required (e.g. the subject of a verb has to be a noun) the number of successful applications increases, although we may find cases where the constraints prevent the correct application (e.g. low recall).

In the absence of a data set where we can empirically estimate precision and recall of rule application, we have approximated the ideal context on the basis of linguistic intuitions. More specifically, for different syntactic heads of the rules, we define the most appropriate syntactic constraints through a search algorithm over the syntactic tree produced on T and H (see Section 4.4 for a detailed explanation).

4 Entailment rules acquisition

In the next sections, the steps for the acquisition of rules from Wikipedia pairs are described in detail.

4.1 Step 1: preprocessing Wikipedia dumps

We downloaded two dumps of the English Wikipedia (one dated 6.03.2009, *Wiki 09*, and one dated 12.03.2010, *Wiki 10*).[4] We used the script *WikiExtractor.py*[5] to extract plain text from Wikipedia pages, discarding any other information or annotation, but keeping the reference to the original document. For our goal, we consider only non-identical documents present in both *Wiki 09* and *Wiki 10* (i.e. 1,540,870 documents).

4.2 Step 2: extraction of entailment pairs

For both *Wiki 09* and *Wiki 10* each document has been sentence-splitted, and the sentences of the two versions have been aligned to create pairs. To measure the similarity between the sentences in each pair, we adopted the *Position Independent Word Error Rate (PER)* (Tillmann *et al.*, 1997), a metric based on the calculation of the number of words which differ between a pair of sentences (*diff* function in (1)). Such measure is based on Levenshtein distance, but works at word level, and allows for reordering of words and sequences of words between the two texts (e.g. a translated text *s* and a reference translation *r*). It is expressed by the formula:

$$PER(s, r) = \frac{diff(s,r) + diff(r,s)}{\|r\|} \qquad (1)$$

[4]http://en.wikipedia.org/wiki/Wikipedia:Database_download

[5]http://medialab.di.unipi.it/wiki/Wikipedia_Extractor

Pairs are clustered according to different thresholds:

- Pairs composed by identical sentences were discarded; if only one word was different in the two sentences, we checked if it was a typo correction using (Damerau, 1964) distance. If that was the case, we discarded such pairs as well.
- Pairs in which one of the sentences contains the other one, meaning that the users added some information to the new version, without modifying the old one (set *a*: 1,547,415 pairs).
- Pairs composed by very similar sentences, where users carried out minor editing ($PER < 0.2$) (set *b*: 1,053,114 pairs). We filtered out pairs where differences were correction of misspelling and typos, and two-word sentences.
- Pairs composed by sentences where major editing was carried out ($0.2 < PER < 0.6$), but still describe the same event (set *c*: 2,566,364).
- Pairs in which the similarity between sentences is low ($PER > 0.6$) were discarded.

To extract entailment rules, we consider only the pairs contained in *set b*. For each pair, we intuitively set the sentence extracted from *Wiki 10* as the Text, since we assume that it contains more (and more precise) information w.r.t. the sentence extracted from *Wiki 09*. We set the sentence extracted from *Wiki 09* as the Hypothesis (see Examples 2 and 3).

Example 2.

T: *The Oxford Companion to Philosophy says "there is no single defining position that all anarchists hold [...]"*
H: *According to the Oxford Companion to Philosophy "there is no single defining position that all anarchists hold [...] "*

Example 3.

T: *Bicycles are used by all socio-economic groups because of their convenience [...].*
H: *Bicycles are used by all socio-economic groups due to their convenience [...].*

4.3 Step 3: extraction of entailment rules

Pairs in *set b* are collected in a data set, and processed with the Stanford parser (Klein and Manning,

2003); chunks are extracted from each pair using the script *chunklink.pl*.[6] The assumption underlying our approach is that the difference between T and H (i.e. the editing made by the user on a specific structure) can be extracted from such pairs and identified as an entailment rule. The *rule extraction* algorithm was implemented to this purpose. In details, for each sentence pair the algorithm iteratively compares the chunks of T and H to extract the ones that differ. It can be the case that several chunks of H are identical to a given chunk of T, as in:

```
T:<NP>[The DT][Oxford NNP][Companion NNP]
 </NP><PP>[to TO]</PP> <NP>[Philosophy NNP]
 </NP><VP>[says VBZ]</VP>...

H:<PP>[According VBG]</PP><PP>[to TO]</PP>
 <NP>[the DT][Oxford NNP][Companion NNP]</NP>
 <PP>[to TO]</PP><NP>[Philosophy NNP]</NP>...
```

Therefore, to decide for instance which chunk `<PP>[to TO]</PP>` from H corresponds to the identical chunk in T, the algorithm checks if the previous chunks are equal as well. If this is the case, such chunks are matched. In the example above, the second chunk `<PP>to</PP>` from H is considered as a good match because previous chunks in T and H are equal as well (`<NP>the Oxford Companion</NP>`). If the previous chunks in T and H are not equal, the algorithm keeps on searching. If such match is not found, the algorithm goes back to the first matching chunk and couples the chunk from T with it. Rules are created setting the unmatched chunks from T as the left-hand side of the rule, and the unmatched chunks from H as the right-hand side of the rule. Two consecutive chunks (different in T and H) are considered part of the same rule. For instance, from Examples 2 and 3:

2) `<LHS> says </LHS>`
`<RHS> according to </RHS>`

3) `<LHS> because of </LHS>`
`<RHS> due to </RHS>`

On the contrary, two non consecutive chunks generate two different entailment rules.

[6]http://ilk.uvt.nl/team/sabine/chunklink/README.html

4.4 Step 4: rule expansion with minimal context

As introduced before, our work aims at providing precise and context-rich entailment rules, to maximize their correct application to RTE pairs. So far, rules extracted by the rule extraction algorithm (Section 4.3) are too general with respect to our goal.

To add the minimum context to each rule (as discussed in Section 3), we implemented a *rule expansion* algorithm: both the file with the syntactic representation of the pairs (obtained with the Stanford parser), and the file with the rules extracted at Step 3 are provided as input. For every pair, and separately for T and H, the words isolated in the corresponding rule are matched in the syntactic tree of that sentence, and the common subsumer node is detected. Different strategies are applied to expand the rule, according to linguistic criteria. In details, if the common subsumer node is *i)* a Noun Phrase (NP) node, the rule is left as it is; *ii)* a Prepositional Phrase node (PP), all the terminal nodes of the subtree below PP are extracted; *iii)* a clause introduced by a subordinating conjunction (SBAR), all the terminal nodes of the subtree below SBAR are extracted; *iv)* an adjectival node (ADJP), all the terminal nodes of the tree below the ADJP node are extracted; *v)* a Verbal Phrase node (VP), the dependency tree under the VP node is extracted.

For Example 3 (see Figure 1), the LHS of the rule *because of* is matched in the syntactic tree of T and the prepositional phrase (PP) is identified as common subsumer node. All the terminal nodes and the PoS of the tree below PP are then extracted. The same is done for the RHS of the rule, where the common subsumer node is an adjectival phrase (ADJP).

5 Experiments and results

In the previous section, we described the steps carried out to acquire context-rich entailment rules from Wikipedia revisions. To show the applicability of the adopted methodology, we have performed two experiments focusing, respectively, on entailment rules for *causality* and *temporal expressions*. In particular, as case studies we chose two seeds: the conjunction *because* to derive rules for causality, and the preposition *before* for temporal expressions.

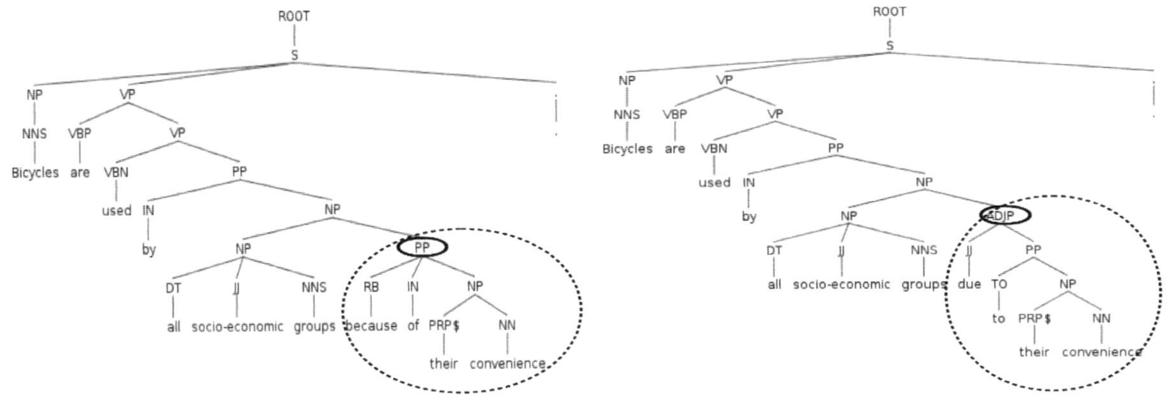

(a) LHS rule

(b) RHS rule

Figure 1: Rule expansion with minimal context (Example 3)

causality (*because*)	**temporal exp. (*before*)**
(PP (RB because) (IN of) (NP (JJ) (NNS)) ⇒ (ADJP (JJ due) (PP (TO to) (NP (JJ) (NNS)))) e.g.: *because of contractual conflicts ⇒ due to contractual conflicts*	(SBAR (IN before) (S)) ⇒ (ADVP (RB prior) (PP (TO to) (S) e.g.: *before recording them ⇒ prior to recording them*
(SBAR (IN because) (S)) ⇒ (VP (PP (IN on) (NP (DT the) (NNS grounds))) (SBAR (IN that) (S) e.g.: *because it penalized people ⇒ on the grounds that it penalized people*	(ADVP (RB prior) (PP (TO to) (NP (DT) (NN)))) ⇒ (SBAR (IN before) (NP (DT) (NN))) e.g.: *prior to the crash ⇒ before the crash*
(PP (RB because) (IN of) (NP (DT) (NN))) ⇒ (PP (IN as) (NP (NP (DT a) (NN result)) (PP (IN of) (NP (DT) (NN))))) e.g.: *because of an investigation ⇒ as a result of an investigation*	(SBAR (IN until) (NP (CD))) ⇒ (SBAR (IN before) (NP (CD))) e.g.: *until 1819 ⇒ before 1819*

Table 1: Sample of extracted entailment rules.

Accordingly, we extracted from *set b* only the pairs containing one of these two seeds (either in T or in H) and we built two separate data sets for our experiments. We run the rule extraction algorithm, and then we filtered again the rules acquired, to collect only those containing one of the two seeds (either in the LHS or in the RHS). This second filtering has been done because there could be pairs in which either *because* or *before* are present, but the differences in T and H do not concern those seeds. The algorithm for rule expansion has then been applied to the selected rules to add the minimal context. The resulting rule for Example 3 is:

```
<rule ruleid="23" docid="844" pairid="15">
<LHS> (PP
      (RB  8 because) (IN 9 of)(NP
           (PRP 10 their)
           (NN 11 convenience))) </LHS>
<RHS> (ADJP
      (JJ  8 due)(PP
           (TO 9 to) (NP
                (PRP 10 their)
                (NN 11 convenience)))) </RHS>
</rule>
```

To create entailment rules balancing high-precision with their recall (Section 3), when the words of the context added to the rule in Step 4 are identical we substitute them with their PoS. For Example 3, the rule is generalized as follows:

```
<rule ruleid="23" docid="844" pairid="15">
<LHS> (PP
      (RB because) (IN of)(NP
           (PRP)
           (NN))) </LHS>
<RHS> (ADJP
      (JJ due)(PP
           (TO to) (NP
                (PRP)
                (NN)))) </RHS>
</rule>
```

The intuition underlying the generalization phase is to allow a more frequent application of the rule, while keeping some constraints on the allowed context. The application of the rule from Example 3 is allowed if the subtrees below the seed words are the same (the rule can be applied in another T-H pair as, e.g. *because of his status* ⇒ *due to his status*).

Contradictions (e.g. antonyms and semantic oppositions) are generally very infrequent, but in certain cases they can have high impact (one of the most frequent rule collected for temporal expression is *before S* ⇒ *after S*). For this reason, we used WordNet (Fellbaum, 1998) to identify and filter antonyms out during the generalization phase. We also checked for awkward inconsistencies due to mistakes of the algorithm on noisy Wikipedia data (e.g. rules with the same seed word in both the LHS and the RHS), and we automatically filtered them out. Table 1 reports a sample of rules extracted for each seed word. Statistics about the resulting data sets, i.e. the number of acquired rules both before and after the generalization phase are shown in Table 2. Identical rules are collapsed into a unique one, but the value of their frequency is kept in the header of that rule. Such index can then be used to estimate the correctness of the rule and, according to our intuition, the probability that the rule preserves the entailment relation.[7]

	causality	temporal exp.
# rules before gen.	1671	813
# rules after gen.	**977**	**457**
rules frequency ≥ 2	66	27

Table 2: Resulting sets of entailment rules

5.1 Evaluation

Due to the sparseness of the phenomena under consideration (i.e. causality and temporal expressions) in RTE data sets, evaluating the acquired rules on such data does not provide interesting results.

For this reason, (following (Zhao *et al.*, 2009), (Callison-Burch, 2008), (Szpektor *et al.*, 2004)), we opted for a manual analysis of a sample of 100 rules per set, including all the rules whose frequency is $\geq$2 (Table 2), plus a random set of rules with frequency equal to 1. Two annotators with skills in linguistics annotated such rules according to five possible values (rules have been presented with the sentence pairs from which they have been acquired): *entailment=yes* (YES), i.e. correctness of the rule; *entailment=more-phenomena* (+PHEN), i.e. the rule is correct, but more than one phenomenon is involved, see Section 5.2; *entailment=unknown* (UNK), i.e. there is no entailment between the LHS and the RHS of the rule, often because the editing changed the semantics of the proposition; *entailment=unknown:reverse_entailment* (REV), wrong directionality, i.e. the RHS of the rule entails the LHS; *entailment=error* (ERR), i.e. the rule is wrong, either because the editing in *Wiki10* was done to correct mistakes, or because the rule is not well-formed due to mistakes produced by our algorithm.

The inter-annotator agreement has been calculated, counting when judges agree on the assigned value. It amounts to 80% on the sample of rules for causality, and to 77% on the sample of rules for temporal expressions. The highest inter-annotator agreement is for correct *entailment* rules, whereas the lowest agreement rates are for *unknown* and *error* judgments. This is due to the fact that detecting correct rules is straightforward, while it is less clear whether to consider a wrong rule as well-formed but with an *unknown* judgment, or to consider it as not appropriate (i.e. *error*). Table 3 shows the outcomes of the analysis of the two sets of rules, as resulting after a reconciliation phase carried out by the annotators. Such results, provided both for the whole samples[8] and for the rules whose frequency is $\geq$2 only, are discussed in the next section.

		YES	+PHEN	UNK	REV	ERR
caus.	all	67	2	13	8	10
	fr$\geq$2	80.3	0	16.7	1.5	1.5
temp.	all	36	6	23	7	28
	fr$\geq$2	52	3.7	37	7.3	0

Table 3: Accuracy (%) of the extracted sets of rules.

5.2 Discussion and error analysis

Due to the amount of noisy data present in Wikipedia, on average 19% of the collected rules

[7]It is difficult to compare our results with related work, since such phenomena are not covered by other resources. The correct comparison would be with the subset of e.g. DIRT paraphrases dealing with causality and temporal relations, if any.

[8]We are aware of the fact that including all the most frequent rules in the sample biases the results upwards, but our choice is motivated by the fact that we aim at verifying that with redundancy the accuracy is actually improved.

include editing done by the users for spelling and typos corrections, or are just spam (Table 3). To discard such cases, spell-checkers or dictionary-based filters should be used to improve our filtering techniques. Moreover, to select only reliable rules we consider making use of their frequency in the data to estimate the confidence that a certain rule maintains the entailment. The accuracy of the rules occurring more than once is indeed much higher than the accuracy estimated on the whole sample. Also the percentage of incorrect rules is strongly reduced when considering redundant rules. Our assumption about the directionality of entailment rules extracted from Wikipedia versions is also verified (less than 10% of the rules per set are tagged as *reverse-entailment*).

However, since the acquisition procedure privileges precision, only a few rules appear very frequently (Table 2), and this can be due to the constraints defined for the context extraction. This fact motivates also the lower precision of the rules for temporal expressions, where 73% of the sample we analyzed involved rules with frequency equal to 1. Moreover, in most of the rules annotated as *unknown*, the editing of *Wiki10* changed the semantics of the pair, e.g. *before 1990* $\Rightarrow$ *1893*, or *when x produced* $\Rightarrow$ *because x produced*. Further strategies to empirically estimate precision and recall of rule application should be experimented as future work. Indeed, several rules appearing only once represent correct rules, and should not be discarded a priori.

Finally, the idea of using only very similar pairs to extract entailment rules is based on the assumption that such rules should concern one phenomenon at a time (Bentivogli *et al.*, 2010). Despite the strategies adopted to avoid multiple phenomena per rule, in about 10% of the cases two phenomena (e.g lexical and syntactic) are collapsed on consecutive tokens, making it complex to separate them automatically: e.g. in *because of his divorce settlement cost* $\Rightarrow$ *due to the cost of his divorces settlement*, the causative (*because of x* $\Rightarrow$ *due to x*) and the argument realization (*x cost* $\Rightarrow$ *cost of x*) rules should be separated.

6 Conclusion and future work

We have presented a methodology for the automatic acquisition of entailment rules from Wikipedia revision pairs. The main benefits are the following: *i)* potential large-scale acquisition, given the increasing size of Wikipedia revisions; *ii)* new coverage, because Wikipedia revisions contain linguistic phenomena (e.g. causality, temporal expressions), which are not covered by existing resources: as a consequence, the coverage of current TE systems can be significantly extended; *iii)* quality: we introduce the notion of context of a rule as the minimal set of syntactic features maximizing its successful application, and we have implemented it as a search over the syntactic representation of revision pairs.

Results obtained on two experimental acquisitions on causality and temporal expressions (seeds *because* and *before*) show both good quality and coverage of the extracted rules. The obtained resources[9]: *i)* cover entailment and paraphrasing aspects not represented in other similar sets of rules, *ii)* can be easily extended by applying the algorithms to automatically collect rules for other phenomena relevant to inference; and *iii)* are periodically updated, as Wikipedia revisions change continuously. We consider such aspects as part of our future work.

These results encourage us to further improve the approach, considering a number of directions. First, we plan to improve our filtering techniques to exclude revision pairs containing more than one phenomenon considering the syntactic structure of the sentence. Moreover, we are planning to carry out more extended evaluations, according to two possible strategies: *i)* applying the instance-based approach (Szpektor *et al.*, 2007) on the Penn Treebank data (i.e. for each PTB sentence that contains the LHS of an entailment rule from our set, a pair sentence will be generated by replacing the LHS of the rule with its RHS. Human judges will then judge each pair); *ii)* integrating the extracted rules into existing TE systems. However, this evaluation has to be carefully designed, as the ablation tests carried on at the RTE challenges show. In particular, as RTE tasks are moving towards real applications (e.g. summarization) we think that knowledge reflecting real textual variations produced by humans (as opposed to knowledge derived from linguistic resources) may introduce interesting and novel hints.

[9]Available at `http://www.aclweb.org/aclwiki/index.php?title=Textual_Entailment_Resource_Pool`. We encourage its integration into TE systems, to obtain feedback on its utility in TE tasks.

Acknowledgments

This work has been partially supported by the EC-funded project EXCITEMENT (FP7 ICT-287923).

References

Roni Ben Aharon, Idan Szpektor, Ido Dagan. 2010. *Generating Entailment Rules from FrameNet.* Proceedings of the ACL 2010 Conference Short Papers. July 11-16. Uppsala, Sweden.

Regina Barzilay, Lillian Lee. 2003. *Learning to Paraphrase: An Unsupervised Approach Using Multiple-Sequence Alignment.* Proceedings of the HLT-NAACL. May 27-June 1. Edmonton, Canada.

Luisa Bentivogli, Peter Clark, Ido Dagan, Hoa T. Dang, Danilo Giampiccolo. 2010. *The Sixth PASCAL Recognizing Textual Entailment Challenge.* Proceedings of the TAC 2010 Workshop on TE. November 15-16. Gaithersburg, Maryland.

Luisa Bentivogli, Elena Cabrio, Ido Dagan, Danilo Giampiccolo, Medea Lo Leggio, Bernardo Magnini. 2010. *Building Textual Entailment Specialized Data Sets: a Methodology for Isolating Linguistic Phenomena Relevant to Inference.* Proceedings of the Seventh conference on International Language Resources and Evaluation. May 19-21. Malta.

Chris Callison-Burch. 2008. *Syntactic constraints on paraphrases extracted from parallel corpora.* Proceedings of the Conference on Empirical Methods in Natural Language Processing (EMNLP2008) October 25-27. Honolulu, Hawaii.

Ido Dagan, Bill Dolan, Bernardo Magnini, Dan Roth. 2009. *Recognizing textual entailment: Rational, evaluation and approaches.* Natural Language Engineering (JNLE). Special Issue 04, volume 15, i-xvii. Cambridge University Press.

Fred J. Damerau. 1964. *A technique for computer detection and correction of spelling errors.* Commun. ACM, 7 (3), pages 171–176. ACM, New York, NY, USA.

Camille Dutrey, Houda Bouamor, Delphine Bernhard and Aurelien Max 2011. *Local modifications and paraphrases in Wikipedia's revision history.* SEPLN journal (Revista de Procesamiento del Lenguaje Natural), 46:51-58.

Christiane Fellbaum. 1998. *WordNet: An Electronic Lexical Database.* Language, Speech and Communication. MIT Press.

Adrian Iftene, Mihai-Alex Moruz. 2010. *UAIC Participation at RTE-6.* Proceedings of the TAC 2010 Workshop on TE. November 15-16. Gaithersburg, Maryland.

Dan Klein, Christopher D. Manning. 2003. *Accurate Unlexicalized Parsing.* Proceedings of the 41st Meeting of the Association for Computational Linguistics. July 7-12. Sapporo, Japan.

Dekang Lin, Patrick Pantel. 2001. *Discovery of Inference Rules for Question Answering.* Natural Language Engineering 7(4):343-360.

Rowan Nairn, Cleo Condoravdi, Lauri Karttunen. 2006. *Computing relative polarity for textual inference.* Inference in Computational Semantics (ICoS-5). April 20-21. Buxton, UK.

Aurelien Max, Guillaume Wisniewski. 2010. *Mining naturally-occurring corrections and paraphrases from wikipedia's revision history.* Proceedings of the Seventh conference on International Language Resources and Evaluation. May 19-21. Valletta, Malta.

Yashar Mehdad, Matteo Negri, Elena Cabrio, Milen Kouylekov, Bernardo Magnini. 2009. *Using Lexical Resources in a Distance-Based Approach to RTE.* Proceedings of the TAC 2009 Workshop on TE. November 17. Gaithersburg, Maryland.

Shachar Mirkin, Roy Bar-Haim, Jonathan Beran, Ido Dagan, Eyal Shnarch, Asher Stern, Idan Szpektor. 2009. *Addressing Discourse and Document Structure in the RTE Search Task.* Proceedings of the TAC 2009 Workshop on TE. November 17. Gaithersburg, Maryland.

Rani Nelken, Elif Yamangil. 2008. *Mining Wikipedia's Article Revision History for Training Computational Linguistics Algorithms.* Proceedings of the AAAI Workshop on Wikipedia and Artificial Intelligence. July 13-14, Chicago, Illinois.

Satoshi Sekine. 2005. *Automatic Paraphrase Discovery based on Context and Kwywords between NE Pairs.* Proceedings of the International Workshop on Paraphrasing (IWP-05). October 14. Jeju Island, South Korea.

Idan Szpektor, Hristo Tanev, Ido Dagan, Bonaventura Coppola. 2004. *Scaling Web-based Acquisition of Entailment Relations.* Proceedings of the 2004 Conference on Empirical Methods in Natural Language Processing. July 25-26. Barcelona, Spain.

Idan Szpektor, Ido Dagan. 2008. *Learning Entailment Rules for Unary Templates.* Proceedings of the 22nd International Conference on Computational Linguistics (Coling 2008). August 18-22. Manchester, UK.

Idan Szpektor, Eyal Shnarch, Ido Dagan. 2007. *Instance-based Evaluation of Entailment Rule Acquisition.* Proceedings of the 45th Annual Meeting of the Association of Computational Linguistics. June 23-30. Prague, Czech Republic.

Christoph Tillmann, Stephan Vogel, Hermann Ney, Alex Zubiaga, Hassan Sawaf. 1997. *Accelerated DP based search for statistical translation.* Proceedings of the European Conf. on Speech Communication and Technology, pages 26672670. September. Rhodes, Greece.

Mark Yatskar, Bo Pang, Cristian Danescu-Niculescu-Mizil, Lillian Lee. 2010. *For the sake of simplicity: Unsupervised extraction of lexical simplifications from Wikipedia.* Proceedings of the NAACL, pp. 365-368, 2010. Short paper. June 1-6. Los Angeles, USA.

Fabio Massimo Zanzotto, Marco Pennacchiotti. 2010. *Expanding textual entailment corpora from Wikipedia using co-training.* Proceedings of the COLING-Workshop on The Peoples Web Meets NLP: Collaboratively Constructed Semantic Resources. August 28. Beijing, China.

Shiqi Zhao, Haifeng Wang, Ting Liu, Sheng Li. 2009. *Extracting Paraphrase Patterns from Bilingual Parallel Corpora.* Journal of Natural Language Engineering, 15 (4): 503:526.